# 中英对照
# 鲁迅旧体诗

寇志明 译　黄乔生 编

北方联合出版传媒（集团）
股份有限公司
春风文艺出版社
·沈阳

ⓒ 黄乔生　寇志明　2016

#### 图书在版编目（CIP）数据

中英对照鲁迅旧体诗/黄乔生编；寇志明译. —沈阳：春风文艺出版社，2016.12（2021.1重印）
ISBN 978-7-5313-5086-6

Ⅰ.①中… Ⅱ.①黄… ②寇… Ⅲ.①鲁迅诗歌—文学翻译—研究—汉、英 Ⅳ.①I210.5

中国版本图书馆CIP数据核字（2016）第178064号

ZHONGYING DUIZHAO LUXUN JIUTISHI
中英对照鲁迅旧体诗

| | |
|---|---|
| 责任编辑 | 姚宏越 |
| 责任校对 | 潘晓春 |
| 装帧设计 | 张　胜 |
| 幅面尺寸 | 142mm×210mm |
| 字　　数 | 200千字 |
| 印　　张 | 6.25 |
| 版　　次 | 2016年12月第1版 |
| 印　　次 | 2021年1月第2次 |
| 出版发行 | 北方联合出版传媒（集团）股份有限公司<br>春风文艺出版社 |
| 地　　址 | 沈阳市和平区十一纬路25号 |
| 邮　　编 | 110003 |
| 网　　址 | www.chinachunfeng.net |
| 购书热线 | 024-23284402 |
| 印　　刷 | 永清县晔盛亚胶印有限公司 |

ISBN 978-7-5313-5086-6　　　　　　　定价：55.00元

版权专有　侵权必究　举报电话：024-23284391
如有质量问题，请与印刷厂联系调换。联系电话：024-23284384

# 一个国外鲁迅研究者之路（代序）

寇志明

郭沫若为1961年版《鲁迅诗稿》作序，第一句是："鲁迅无心作诗人，偶有所作，每臻绝唱。"一般来讲，我不大认同郭沫若对鲁迅的看法，但愈读鲁迅的诗歌，就愈欣赏这句话。其实，我读鲁迅的其他作品，也一样觉得"每臻绝唱"。

我在美国宾夕法尼亚州的一个与世隔绝的小镇读中学的时候，因为偶尔翻了一下埃德加·斯诺（Edgar Snow）的《大河彼岸》（*The Other Side of the River*）一书后面的参考书目，才知道鲁迅的名字，而且觉得《阿Q正传》这个篇名很新奇：怎么会叫"阿Q"呢？不久我有幸从旧金山中国图书期刊书店邮购到鲁迅的英文短篇小说和杂文集。我阅读的是杨宪益和他的妻子戴乃迭的译文，北京外文出版社出版。

高中毕业，我在匹兹堡大学修中文暑期班，很巧我的第一位汉语老师是台益坚先生——原来是鲁迅的学生台静农的长子！有一天我提了鲁迅的名字，他很惊讶，并说他父亲认识鲁迅，他很小的时候，鲁迅到过他们家。有一次鲁迅不小心，把手中的热茶倒在他身上。我说："我不相信！"没想到，他居然解开衬衫，说:"我还有一个疤。"我就连忙说:"不!老师不用脱!"因为当时美国俚语里讲"我不相信",意思只不过是"可不是吗!"是用来加强"太巧"的语气。

另外,我记得我曾经请教过他关于《狂人日记》里"吃人"的象征意义。我当时以为指的是帝国主义要瓜分中国。台先生笑了,说:"不是。那是指中国社会里一些人。"但可惜他没有多说。我估计是由于当时中美还处于冷战状态,他觉得这个题目不大好在汉语课里讲。

后来,我到纽约哥伦比亚大学主修中国语文及文化,在夏志清教授(1921—2013)的指导下读中国新、旧文学。虽然他的《现代中国小说史》有一章论述鲁迅,但在课堂上他极少讲鲁迅,只说"鲁迅是一个 dilettante(有文化的大闲人),天天到一家日本书店度过午后时光"。后来我自己看书才知道鲁迅到内山书店拿信、会客,跟他的工作和身份有关。

哥大毕业后我到台湾去深造两年。当时是国民党统治下的"戒严"时期,鲁迅以及大多数五四时代作家的著作〔除了徐志摩(1897—1931)与朱自清(1898—1948)以外〕被禁止阅读。不过我从香港带回"姜添"编的那本薄薄的《鲁迅诗注析》(即江天的"红卫兵"内部发行的《鲁迅诗新解》,香港编辑删除了关于阶级斗争等内容)。这本书注释不多,但多强调革命和阶级斗争。我一首一首地慢慢读下去,对鲁迅的诗感到兴趣,也受到挑战。但这本书留给我的问题多于答案。

第二年我有幸拿到了美国国会所办的东西文化中心的奖学金,到了夏威夷大学,在罗锦堂老师指导下修中国文学硕士课程。我把鲁迅的旧体诗研究作为论文题目,不过我当时也对受过鲁迅影响的台湾乡土作家陈映真(1937— )的作品感兴趣。我后来到加州伯克利大学读完博士课程，在北京大学跟《野草》研究专家孙玉石进修，再以后，回到伯克利，在白之（Cyril Birch）教授指导下写了一本关于清末民初的旧派诗人王闿运（1833—1916）、樊增祥（1846—1931）、易顺鼎（1858—1920）、陈三立（1852—1937）、陈衍（1856—1937）以及郑孝胥（1860—1938）的博士论文。这个题目跟我的硕士论文题目很不一样，因为这几位诗人的思想与诗作和鲁迅迥然不同。不过，他们之间也有共同点，即如何用旧体诗这个"古典形式"来表达现代意识。

博士毕业以后，我对原来的鲁迅诗无韵译文做了几次修改，出版了《诗人鲁迅：关于其旧体诗的研究》（*The Lyrical Lu Xun: a Study of his Classical-style Verse*）一书，包含题解、直译、押韵译文以及详注等部分。很遗憾我当时没有亲自向在台湾军政体制下生活了几十年的台静农先生请教过。因为台教授在新中国成立前的大陆坐过监狱，加之鲁迅的朋友、担任过中国台湾大学中文系主任的许寿裳在1948年被暗杀了，我听说台先生不敢讲关于鲁迅的事情，我也担心给他带来麻烦。但过了些年，台湾快要解严的时候，我通过老师罗锦堂，请台先生为我的书《诗人鲁迅》（*The Lyrical Lu Xun*）题写了书名。

虽然这些年来我的研究方向发生过多次变化，但是我对鲁迅作品的兴趣从未衰退，我一直热衷于探索他作品中未翻译成英文或者研究得比较少的部分，我因此从鲁迅的旧体诗走向他的早期文言论文。这些文章同他的旧体诗一样虽然是用古文写的，但在内容上却有明显的现代性倾向。我当初的另一个想法是鲁迅用旧体诗写作可能会更容易把他的个人情怀通过旧形式和在中国文化中受尊敬的古语文、典故等表达出来。在鲁迅的旧体诗中，我们看到一个无畏地批判军阀和后来的国民党白色恐怖政权的批评家，但同时我们也能发现一位关心学生的好老师，爱孩子的家长，爱妻子的丈夫，一位人道主义者，爱国学者和一位具有国际主义精神的、胸襟博大的诗人；他怀有悲悯和失落的强烈情感，但从未对中国未来丧失希望。

非常感激黄乔生先生以及出版社提供这个机会让中国国内读者看到我的译文。这些译文最初是我的英文专著《诗人鲁迅：关于其旧体诗的研究》（*The Lyrical Lu Xun*）（檀香山：夏威夷大学出版社，1996年）的一部分。可惜该书一直没有在中国发行过。

关于我翻译与阐释鲁迅旧体诗的方法，读者可以参考我在美国《中国文学》（*Chinese Literature: Essays, Articles, Reviews*）学报上发表的几篇评论文章。其中有一些现在也可以在我的个人网站jonvonkowallis.com上看到。第一篇是《鲁迅的诗》（*Poems of Lu Hsun*，第3卷，183—188页）。第二篇是《鲁迅的旧体诗》（*Lu Xun's Classical Poetry*，第13卷，101—118页）；第三篇是《解读鲁迅》（*Interpreting Lu Xun*，第18卷，153—164页）。其中大部分已被翻译为中文，发表在北京鲁迅博物馆编的《鲁迅研究月刊》上。其中有一篇《鲁迅旧体诗注释与英译略述》（载《鲁迅研究月刊》2004年第4期，72—82页），译自英文《中国文学》上的《鲁迅的旧体诗》一文，由黄乔生译为中文，还有发表在《鲁迅研究月刊》（2002年第1期，37—48页）上的《鲁迅："释"与"译"》，则是《中国文学》上的《解读鲁迅》（*Interpreting Lu Xun*）的中译，评论的是顾彬（Wolfgang Kubin）的德文翻译。这些文章反映我关于鲁迅诗歌翻译的思考，也涉及20世纪40年代以来鲁迅旧体诗诠释中存在的若干问题。另外，我还用中文写了一篇关于我在海外研究鲁迅的心得体会的文章，发表在《上海鲁迅研究》(2007年春，66—81页)。

最近中国高等教育出版社出版了英文学报 Frontiers of Literary Studies in China（《中国文学研究前沿》）。我为他们编一本关于鲁迅与章太炎（1868—1936）的特号（即2013年9月，第7卷，3号，422—440页），收录了我的一篇讨论《摩罗诗力说》英文翻译问题的文章。关于英语世界鲁迅研究动态我有两篇文章：一篇是用中文发表的《鲁迅研究在英语世界：过去，当前，未来》，收入《鲁迅社会影响调查报告》一书（人民日报出版社，2011年，257—276页）——可惜中文编辑把文中所有的英文书名都删掉了，因而减少了这篇文字的参考价值。另外一篇是我最近用英文写的《我们心目中的鲁迅：后社会主义时期西方对鲁迅的重新评价》（Lu Xun on Our Minds: The Post-Socialist Reappraisal），发表于美国《亚洲研究》季刊（The Journal of Asian Studies）第73卷，第3号（2014年8月，1—7页）。在那篇文章里我讨论了最近几年在西方（美国、英国、澳大利亚）突然兴起的"鲁迅热"，介绍了2009年以来出版的六本新书：周珊（Eva Shan Chou）著《记忆、暴力、辫子：鲁迅对中国的解读》（Memory, Violence, Queues: Lu Xun Interprets China，密歇根，安阿伯：亚洲研究协会2012年）；格洛丽娅·戴维斯（Gloria Davies）著《鲁迅的革命：在一个充满暴力时代写作》（Lu Xun's Revolution: Writing in a Time of Violence，麻省，剑桥：哈佛大学出版社，2013年）；郑爱玲（Eileen Cheng）著《文学遗产：死亡、心灵创伤，以及鲁迅如何拒绝哀痛》（Literary Remains: Death, Trauma and Lu Xun's Refusal to Mourn，檀香山：夏威夷大学出版社，2013年）；尼古拉斯·卡拉蒂斯（Nicholas Kaldis）著《中文散文诗：关于鲁迅〈野草〉的研究》（The Chinese Prose Poem: A Study of Lu Xun's Wild

*Grass: Yecao*），纽约州：卡恩布里亚出版社，2014年）；安德鲁·琼斯（Andrew Jones）著《为促进成长的童话：进化论式的思想与现代中国文化》（*Developmental Fairy Tales: Evolutionary Thinking and Modern Chinese Culture*，哈佛大学出版社，2011年）；朱丽娅·洛威尔（Julia Lovell）翻译的《〈阿Q正传〉和其他中国故事》（*The Real Story of Ah Q and Other Tales of China*，伦敦：企鹅出版社，2009年）。

目前我正在研究鲁迅早期思想。这个研究项目包括他早期文言论文《摩罗诗力说》《文化偏至论》《破恶声论》以及《拟播布美术意见书》的英译和注释。我认为鲁迅的早期文言论文形成了他整个文学生涯的蓝图。另外我正在编一本英文鲁迅传略和鲁迅学术研究著作书目。在此我想感谢蒋经国基金会、夏威夷大学出版社、加州伯克利大学东亚学院、中国汉办以及澳大利亚学术研究委员会的支持。

2007年8月我接受了强小路（音译）先生的电子邮件采访。他是一位年轻中国留学生，当时在英国谢菲尔德大学翻译研究专业攻读硕士学位。他的硕士论文比较了我和詹纳尔（W.J.F. Jenner）教授翻译的鲁迅旧体诗，后者由北京外文出版社出版，题为《鲁迅诗集》*Lu Xun Selected Poems*（1982）。以下是采访内容：

**1. 问：你翻译诗歌受了什么影响？你最喜欢读什么类型的诗歌？**

答：这是两个独立的问题。我在研究生期间一度花费了一些时间研究附有各类评注的《楚辞》，并把原文与大卫·霍克斯（David Hawkes）和林文庆（Lim Boon Keng）相当"直"的英译本相比较。随后我读了杨宪益夫妇的富有韵律的翻译。虽然我以前曾反对那种过度修饰的翻译方式，但我这才意识到它对传情达意非常有帮助，并能将它融入一种像中古时代英国诗歌一样的形式。我认为它教给了我关于翻译的重要一课：It is not just bringing over the meaning that is important, it is recreating a certain feeling engendered by the original poem（翻译不仅仅是为了表达意义，更要通过重新创造把原诗中特定的情感表达出来）。

我喜欢托马斯·斯特恩·艾略特（T.S. Eliot）、埃兹拉·庞德（Ezra Pound）的作品，还有许多"垮掉的一代"诗人——劳伦斯·弗林盖蒂（Lawrence Ferlinghetti）、艾伦·金斯堡（Allen Ginsberg）、加里·斯奈德（Gary Snyder）、肯尼斯·雷克思罗斯（Kenneth Rexroth）等。同样也喜欢读现代民谣的歌词，如鲍勃·迪伦（Bob Dylan）、伍迪·古德雷（Woody Guthrie）、皮特·西格（Pete Seeger），约翰·列侬（John Lennon）、保罗·西蒙（Paul Simon）、兰迪·纽曼（Randy Newman）等音乐家的歌词也是现代英语诗歌。我也欣赏早期大师的作品——《贝奥武夫》（Beowulf）、乔叟（Chaucer）、莎士比亚（Shakespeare）、拜伦（Byron）、雪莱（Shelly）、济慈（Keats）、埃德加·爱伦·坡（Edgar Allen Poe）等。爱伦·坡的《安娜贝尔·李》（Annabel Lee），凝重而富有音乐性和想象力。我也喜欢中国诗人如杜甫、李白、白居易、李商隐、李贺、苏东坡等。

在我的第二本专著《微妙的革命：清末民初"旧派"诗人》 The Subtle Revolution（伯克利：加利福尼亚大学东亚研究所，中国研究丛书60号，2006年）中，我对王闿运、樊增祥、易顺鼎、陈三立、陈衍和郑孝胥的诗歌做了论述、翻译、分析。我选择这些诗人的动机之一是因为我想了解鲁迅（也就是五四时代作家、诗人）的前辈的作品是怎样的，特别是诗体上保守的而无意于形式创新的诗人（因为诗人黄遵宪积极参与梁启超主张的"诗界革命"，所以我把他当例外，没有对他进行研究。而且北美两三位学者已经出版过关于黄遵宪的学术专著）。在我那本《微妙的革命》中，我也提出了一个问题，即他们这些被陈炳坤称为"旧派"诗人的作品在多大程度上可以蕴含现代性或现代意识。李欧梵早就提出，鲁迅的旧体诗中清晰地存在着现代意识。但别人呢？这就是我在《微妙的革命》中的出发点。鲁迅就更毫无疑问不是在造"假古董"（这是胡适在《五十年来中国之文学》对王闿运的错误批判）。不过话说远了——这是另一本书的主题。

2. 问：你翻译鲁迅旧体诗的方法是什么？

答：我想用英文尝试唤起跟原文所能引起的同样的情感。换句话说，我致力于将原诗的境界融于另一种文化和习俗，同时试图保存原初的画面（即其意象 images）、感觉以及韵律，这些在中国旧体诗中都很重要。

3. 问：对于《诗人鲁迅》书中的译诗，你的目标读者是谁？

答：西方世界中研究中国文学的学者。在这里我指的是：对中国文学和现代思想史感兴趣的专家和学者、研究生和大学生；想深入了解鲁迅的一般英文读者；懂得英语并想进行比较翻译的中国读者以及最近兴起并蓬勃发展的群体——翻译理论的学生。

4. 问：你认为你翻译鲁迅诗歌的最突出特点是什么？

答：努力再现原作的情感和神韵，注重形式和韵律。

**5. 问：你认为在你的诗歌翻译中运用文学手法（如押韵或韵律）有什么重要性？**

答：其中一部分重要性与中国读者和旧体诗作者要求韵律和音调组合（英语可称为诗歌"音乐"the "music" of the poetry）有关。这种优先次序在一定程度上是由文化决定的。但是它对英文读者群也同样重要——一般读者群更希望一首诗"听起来像一首诗"，而不是读起来像散文。但这触发出的问题是不能够满足更多的专业读者。学者不需要韵律，因为他们想更加精确地了解外文诗歌的内容（尽管由于语言和文字的差异我们不可能达到"精确"的翻译，即道出原诗所蕴含的每一种深意）。出于这个原因，我在中国汉字和拼音下面提供了"直译"，紧接着提供一个形象性（即文学性）的"顺译"与大量的注解。我写作《诗人鲁迅》是为了让读者更加"接近"鲁迅的旧体诗——词句解释和意义注解旨在帮助学生读懂原文。大卫·霍克斯（David Hawkes）在他的《杜甫入门》（*A Little Primer of Tu Fu*）中也曾尝试这样做，但是他并没有提供形象性的翻译；相反，他只是把英语译文写成一段散文：没有格律，没有押韵，连诗行都不分——我知道个中原委——但这令很多读者感到失望。

**6. 问：你认为强调韵律会歪曲文意，弱化读者理解吗？**

答：不一定。这部分取决于诗歌本身，部分取决于翻译者的技巧。我发现对这个方法缺乏耐心的人，大部分自诩为美国当代诗人或英美文学专家，而不是普通读者。他们始终拒绝让韵律再进入现代英语诗歌。这来自对现代诗歌美学的一个重新定义。美国内战（中国叫南北战争）期间，很多美国诗人放弃了押韵，因为觉得不自然，太矫揉造作（在英语里押韵的字比较少，所以他们认为知道诗中第一句，韵律是可预见的，也就是说诗中第二句会是什么马上可以猜到的，因而不够现代）。但是，既然我研究中国文学，而不是研究当代美国诗人，我想我可以承担一些美学的风险。乔治·华盛顿大学的乔纳森·查维斯（Jonathan Chaves）也赞同这个立场。我的一个美国诗人朋友查尔斯·贝尔宾（Charles Belbin，现在旧金山城市学院教授英文）曾经说，他认为我通过长期留学、工作在中国而受到过度影响，已经明白了怎样在中国诗歌的翻译中尊重中国式思维。查尔斯的意思是，如果你将中国诗歌译为英文，你需要给英语世界的读者他们期望看到的而不是中国读者期望看到的东西。但是我认为鲁迅大部分旧体诗是在20世纪30年代（他一生最后五六年）中写作的，这是一个我们要考虑的重要因素。他是在用白话写作新体诗以及散文诗《野草》之后才回归旧体诗的。新体诗在闻一多、朱湘、徐志摩、朱自清等的诗歌中已经取得长足进步。从某种意义上说，鲁迅选择旧体诗在形式上是仿古的，他这样做出于各种原因。因此我认为这种现代诗歌的古风应该至少暗示于目标语言（英文）中，那么韵律的使用是合理的。这不同于杜甫和白居易的翻译，因为他们是以他们自己的时代风格写作，所以翻译成英文，用韵律并非必要。事实上，白居易致力于使用俗白、质朴的语言，使得市井上缺乏教育的商贩能理解他口头朗诵的诗歌。而鲁迅的风格则不同，他除了使用古代语言、音调和韵律之外，经常采用象征和高度暗喻的语言。因此，我翻译鲁迅的旧体诗使用英语韵律，而在杜甫和白居易的翻译中却不必如此。在《微妙的革命：清末民初"旧体"诗人》中，我翻译的晚清和民国初期的诗歌就没有运用韵律，因为这些诗人在那个时代还不能算刻意仿古。

**7. 问：你在翻译《无题》（"惯于长夜"）和《悼杨铨》时使用的韵律标准是什么？**

答：杨宪益曾经评论过我的翻译："如果恭维你一句，就是'自成风格'。"随后他用英语说："假如我想称赞你，可以说你已经创造了自己的风格。你不模仿其他人的诗句，或者落入'英雄双韵体'（heroic couplets）的模式，那是其他翻译者常做的事。"

最后我做一个总结：当初我开始研究鲁迅旧体诗的时候，这在西方学术界是一个十分冷门的题目，但最近十几年以来中西学界对鲁迅旧体诗的兴趣越来越大。这对我来说是一种鼓励。在英语世界里，我将自己的热情献给了鲁迅的诗歌以及早期文言论文的翻译。正如鲁迅在《野草》"题辞"中写的那句："地火在地下运行。"我希望拙译也能或多或少为"地火"的燃烧添加燃料——鲁迅也曾预测这地火会喷发的。

从我在美国开始阅读鲁迅到现在，中国已经发生过很多变化。在这个改革开放的过程中，中国走向了世界，鲁迅的著作不但在中国的"精神界"产生了巨大影响，就连国外，知道鲁迅著作的人也越来越多了。鲁迅在《故乡》中告诉我们："地上本没有路，走的人多了，也便成了路。"

2015年3月

# My Road to Lu Xun Research

Jon Eugene von Kowallis

Guo Moruo once observed in a preface he was invited to write for the 1961 edition of the Lu Xun Shigao [Lu Xun's Poetry in His Own Calligraphy] that "Lu Xun never set out to be a poet, but when he did compose poems, each one was exquisite." I've never been one to put much store in Guo Moruo's opinions of Lu Xun, but the more I study Lu Xun's poetry, the more I would concur with that observation. And that holds true for the rest of his works as well.

I first became interested in modern China's foremost author Lu Xun (1881-1936) when I was in high school in a backwater town in Pennsylvania while paging through the bibliography at the back of Edgar Snow's book *The Other Side of the River*, which made mention of someone called "Lu Hsn" and his *True Story of Ah Q*. The name "Ah Q" (and Snow's enthusiastic endorsement of Lu Xun) sparked my curiosity so much so that I chanced to successfully mail order a collection of his short stories and essays, first reading them in English translations done by Yang Xianyi (1915-2009) and his wife Gladys Tayler Yang (1919-1999), published by the Foreign Languages Press in Beijing.

As soon as I had graduated high school I took a summer intensive language course at the University of Pittsburgh and my first Chinese teacher just happened to be Tai Yijian, the son of Lu Xun's own protégé and literary associate Tai Jingnong (1902-1990). He seemed startled one day when I mentioned Lu Xun's name during a break in class — his first reaction was to tell me his father had known Lu Xun and that Lu Xun visited their home when he was small. He quickly added that once Lu Xun had spilled a cup of hot tea on him, at which point I exclaimed: "I don't believe it!" He then began to unbutton his shirt, saying "I still have a scar from it," which he intended to show the class as proof when I hastily interjected: "That's fine. I don't need to see it!" In colloquial American English "I don't believe it!" had the connotation of "That's incredible," emphasizing the rarity of the coincidence.

I also remember asking him about the symbolic meaning of cannibalism in Lu Xun's story Kuangren Riji "Diary of a Madman". At the time I thought it must have referred to the way the imperialist powers wanted to carve up China. I remember that he just laughed and said: "No. It refers to some people in Chinese society." I have always thought it a pity he did not elaborate, but I guess it was because that was still during the Cold War era and he may have thought it inappropriate to go into such a topic in any detail in a Chinese language class.

Later I majored in Chinese language and culture at Columbia University as an undergraduate and studied both modern and traditional Chinese literature under C.T. Hsia (1921-2013). Although his *History of Modern Chinese Fiction* contains a chapter on Lu Xun, Prof. Hsia actually said very little about him in class, other than to remark "Lu Xun was a dilettante. He spent most of his afternoons in a Japanese bookstore." It wasn't until later that I learned from my own reading that Lu Xun received his mail at Uchiyama Kanzo's bookstore and used it as an office to interact with the public. After graduation, I went on to further study in Taiwan, which was then under martial law, and the works of Lu Xun and most other writers of the May Fourth generation were banned, except for Xu Zhimo (1897-1931) and Zhu Ziqing (1898-1948). I first read Lu Xun's poetry, verse by verse, in a slim volume I had brought in from Hong Kong titled Lu Xun Shi Zhu Xi [Lu Xun's Poetry Annotated and Analyzed], attributed to one Jiang Tian (probably a pseudonym - this was a toned-down version of what could have been a Red Guard publication originally attributed to a Jiang Tian 江天 and reprinted in Hong Kong under a slightly different title Lu Xun Shi Xin Jie [New Interpretations of Lu Xun's Poetry]). The latter tended to stress revolutionary and class-struggle angles in its interpretations. I was challenged and intrigued by the poetry but the book left more questions in my mind than it answered.

Fortunately, toward the end of my second year in Taiwan I received a scholarship from the Congressionally-funded East-West

Center, which enabled me to return to the US and continue my study of Chinese literature for a Masters degree at the University of Hawaii under Lo Chin-t'ang. At that time I wrote a thesis on Lu Xun's classical-style poetry, although I was also drawn to the fiction of Chen Yingzhen (b. 1937), a xiangtu (local color) author from Taiwan who influenced by Lu Xun. Later I conducted research at Peking University under Sun Yushi, who had published extensively on Lu Xun's prose poetry collection Yecao (Wild Grass), as part of my PhD program at the University of California, Berkeley, where I eventually completed a dissertation on a very different subject — the Poets of the "Old Schools" during the late-Qing and early Republican eras, supervised by Cyril Birch. These included Wang Kaiyun (1833–1916), Fan Zengxiang (1846–1931), Yi Shunding (1858–1920), Chen Sanli (1856–1937), Chen Yan (1856–1937) and Zheng Xiaoxu (1860–1938). But although their ideas and their poetic compositions were quite different from Lu Xun, there were nevertheless some similarities in terms of the entry of modernity through the vehicle of a classical literary genre.

It was not until after I had revised my original free-verse translations a number times that I published my first monograph *The Lyrical Lu Xun: a Study of his Classical-style Verse*, in which I used both literal glosses, followed by a formal rhyming translation and extensive annotations. Tai Jingnong, who had lived on Taiwan through decades of martial law, was kind enough to write the calligraphy for the title page at my request through Lo Chin-t'ang during the last years of the martial law period. I have always thought it a great pity that I never had a chance to discuss Lu Xun's poetry with Tai Jingnong, but I was reluctant to approach him about a subject he was reluctant to address and which could have caused him problems. Prof. Tai had been jailed several times under the Kuomintang regime on mainland China and his predecessor as head of the Chinese Department at Taiwan University, Xu Shouchang (1883-1948), another friend of Lu Xun, had been murdered under suspicious circumstances in 1948, at the beginning of the martial law period.

Although the topics of my research changed over the years, my interest in Lu Xun never faded and I have always been keen to explore the untranslated or less-studied aspects of his work. That is in part what led me to his classical-style poetry and later his early essays, which were also written in classical Chinese, but have a distinctly modern orientation in terms of content. Another thing I had in mind was the idea that another more intimate and personal aspect of Lu Xun might emerge from his compositions in the old forms and old languages. In his classical poetry we see a defiant critic of the warlord and Kuomintang regimes, but at the same time we also find a concerned teacher, a lover, a family man, a humanist, a patriot-scholar, an internationalist and a poet of great sensibility, with a keen sense of tragedy and loss, but yet never losing hope for the future of China.

I am very grateful to the publishers and the editors, Mr Huang Qiaosheng, Director of the Lu Xun Research Institute in

Beijing, for this opportunity to share my translations of Lu Xun's classical-style poetry with the readership in China, where book publishing continues to flourish in hard copy as well as on the internet. These translations were originally part of a longer monograph titled *The Lyrical Lu Xun: a Study of His Classical-style Verse* (Honolulu: University of Hawaii Press, 1996), which has not had direct distribution in China.

For my detailed thoughts on translating and interpreting Lu Xun's classical-style poetry, I would ask that my readers in China refer to several review articles originally published in the American scholarly journal *Chinese Literature: Essays, Article, Reviews* (CLEAR). A number of these can now be read on my personal website jonvonkowallis.com. The first was titled "Poems of Lu Xun" in CLEAR, vol. 3, pp. 183–188. Next there was "Lu Xun's Classical Poetry" in CLEAR, vol. 13, pp.101–118; A third piece was "Interpreting Lu Xun" in CLEAR, vol. 18, pp. 153–164. Most of them have been translated into Chinese and published in the journal Lu Xun Yanjiu Yuekan [Lu Xun Research Monthly], an organ of the Lu Xun Research Institute affiliated with the Beijing Lu Xun Museum. These are under the titles: Lu Xun Jiutishi Zhushi yu Yingyi Lueshu (An Overview of the Various Exegeses of Lu Xun's Old-style Poetry and Its Translation into English) published in Lu Xun Yanjiu Yuekan, 2004, no. 4, pp. 72–82, being a Chinese translation by Huang Qiaosheng of "Lu Xun's Classical Poetry" which appeared in CLEAR, op. cit.; and Lu Xun 'shi' yu 'yi' (Exegesis versus translation in the study of Lu Xun) in Lu

Xun Yanjiu Yuekan, 2002, no. 1, pp. 37-48 — a Chinese translation of "Interpreting Lu Xun" from CLEAR, op. cit.), which includes my views on Wolfgang Kubin's German translations. The above articles reflect my thoughts and ruminations on a number of the issues involved in translating and interpreting Lu Xun's poetry which have arisen since the first commentaries began in the 1940s. Another article on my experience as a Lu Xun researcher, written in Chinese, appears in the quarterly journal Shanghai Lu Xun Yanjiu [Shanghai Lu Xun Research](Spring 2007), pp. 66-81.

More recently I have edited a special issue of the English-language journal Frontiers of Literary Studies in China, vol. 7, no. 3 (September 2013), which focusses on Lu Xun and his erstwhile teacher Zhang Taiyan (Zhang Binglin, 1869-1936) and contains an article on my reflections on translating Lu Xun's book-length early essay Moluo Shi Li Shuo (*On the Power of Mara Poetry*). I contributed a chapter in Chinese titled Lu Xun Yanjiu zai Yingyu Shijie: Guoqu, Dangqian, Weilai (*Lu Xun Research in the English-speaking world: the past, present and future*) in the book Lu Xun Shehui Yingxiang: Diaocha Baogao (Renmin Ribao Chubanshe, 2011), pp. 257-276, from which an editor unfortunately removed all the original English book titles. My most recent contribution to the field is a review article in English titled *Lu Xun on Our Minds, The Post-Socialist Reappraisal* in the American Journal of Asian Studies, vol. 73, no. 3 (August 2014), pp. 1-7. There I discuss the new wave of enthusiasm for Lu Xun in the West, which has brought about six new books in the last few years: Eva

Shan Chou's *Memory, Violence, Queues: Lu Xun Interprets China* (Ann Arbor, MI: Association for Asian Studies, 2012); Gloria Davies' *Lu Xun's Revolution: Writing in a Time of Violence* (Cambridge, MA: Harvard University Press, 2013); Eileen Cheng's *Literary Remains: Death, Trauma and Lu Xun's Refusal to Mourn* (Honolulu: University of Hawaii Press, 2013); Nicholas Kaldis' *The Chinese Prose Poem: A Study of Lu Xun's Wild Grass* (Amherst, NY: Cambria Sinophone World Series, 2014); as well as related books by Andrew Jones' *Developmental Fairy Tales: Evolutionary Thinking and Modern Chinese Culture* (Harvard University Press, 2011) and Julia Lovell's new translation of Lu Xun's short stories *The Real Story of Ah Q and Other Tales of China* (London: Penguin Classics, 2009). As this is a wholly new phenomenon in Western scholarly publishing, it may well constitute a trend.

My own current research involves the formation of Lu Xun's early thought and this includes the translation and annotation of his early essays Moluo Shi Li Shuo (*On the Power of Mara Poetry*), Wenhua Pianzhi Lun (*On Imbalanced Cultural Development*), Po E'sheng Lun (*Toward a Refutation of Malevolent Voices*) and Ni Bobu Meishu Yijianshu (*A Proposal for the Dissemination of Aesthetic Knowledge*). I am also compiling a research biography and annotated bibliography of Lu Xun Studies done in Chinese, English and Japanese. Here I would like to express my gratitude to the Chiang Ching-kuo Foundation; the East Asian Institute at the University of California, Berkeley; the Han Ban; and the Australian Research Council for their continued support of my various research projects.

The following interview was given by me via email to Qiang Xiaolu in August 2007, then a graduate student in Translation Studies at the University of Sheffield in England, writing an MA thesis that compared my translations in The Lyrical Lu Xun with those done into plain verse by Professor W.J.F. Jenner and published by the Foreign Languages Press in Beijing and published under the title Lu Xun Poems (1982).

Here follows the text of the interview:

**1. QUESTION: What influences have there been on your translations of poetry? What type of poetry do you like to read most?**

ANSWER: These are two separate questions. At one point in my graduate study I spent some time studying the original text of the Chu Ci with various Chinese commentaries and comparing it against the relatively "literal" translations by David Hawkes and Lim Boon Keng (Lin Wenqing). Then I looked at the Yangs' rhyming translation, done into heroic couplets after the style of John Dryden, which I had previously rejected as overly artificial, and realized that it went a long way toward conveying the meaning and putting it into a form that sounded like old English poetry. I think that taught me an important lesson about translation — it's not just bringing over the meaning that is important, it is recreating a certain feeling engendered by the poem.

I like the works of T.S. Eliot, Ezra Pound, some Beat poetry and its antecedents — Lawrence Ferlinghetti, Allen Ginsberg, Gary

Snyder, Kenneth Rexroth, etc., but also modern lyricists like Bob Dylan, Woody Guthrie, Pete Seeger, John Lennon, Paul Simon, Randy Newman, etc. I also appreciate the works of old masters —*Beowulf*, Chaucer, Shakespeare, Byron, Shelly, Keats' Edgar Allan Poe (eg. Poe's '*Annabel Lee*', which is heavy but rich in musical phrases and sensual images) and Chinese poets like Du Fu, Li Bai, Bai Juyi, Li Shangyin, Li He Su Shi (Dongpo), etc.

In my second monograph, *The Subtle Revolution: Poets of the Old Schools during late Qing and early Republican China* (Berkeley: University of California, Institute of East Asian Studies, China Research Monographs no. 60, 2006) I wrote on Wang Kaiyun, Fan Zengxiang, Yi Shunding, Chen Sanli, Chen Yan, and Zheng Xiaoxu. One of my motivations in choosing these poets was that I wanted to know what the works of Lu Xun's predecessors were like, in particular those who were stylistically conservative and did not aim to be innovators in the old forms (not as did poets such as Huang Zunxian, who, together with Liang Qichao, advocated "a revolution in the world of poetics"). In that book I also asked the question of to what extent their works could articulate modernity or a modern consciousness. I think that goes without saying in Lu Xun's classical-style verse — I mean the modern consciousness is clearly there. He certainly wasn't producing jia gudong 假古董 (fake antiques). Neither was Wang Kaiyun, as Hu Shi wrongly charged, but that is the subject of another book.

2. QUESTION: What is your approach to the translation

of Lu Xun's poems, especially his classical-style poems?

ANSWER: I wanted to try and recreate the same feeling in English as the original engenders. In other words, I am striving to bring the "world" (jingjie 境界) of the poem over into another culture and another idiom, while attempting to preserve the original images and the sense of structure and rhyme that are so important to the old forms in Chinese.

3. QUESTION: Who do you see as your target audience for the translations in your book *The Lyrical Lu Xun*?

ANSWER: Scholars of Chinese literature in the West. Here I mean specialists and scholars in general, graduate and undergraduate students interested in Chinese literature and modern intellectual history; general readers of English who may have read his stories but want to know more about Lu Xun; Chinese readers who know English and want to compare translations and finally a new and burgeoning group: students of translation theory.

4. QUESTION: What do you think is the most prominent feature of your translations of the poems of Lu Xun?

ANSWER: The concern with reproducing the "feeling" or atmosphere of the original and the attention to form and rhyme.

5. QUESTION: What do you think of the importance of applying literary devices (like, rhymes & metres) in your poetry translating?

ANSWER: Part of this has to do with the importance attached to rhyme and tonal scheme (let's call that "the music of the poetry" in English) by Chinese readers and writers of classical-style verse. This priority is culturally determined, to a certain extent. But it is also important to the English readership — the general reader will expect a poem to "sound like a poem," not read like prose. But this engenders problems not satisfying more specialized audiences. Scholars don't necessarily want rhyme because they want to know exactly what the poet is saying (although it's often not possible to make an "exact" translation because of the difference in languages as well as words — their implications and shades of meaning). For that reason, I provided literal glosses underneath the Chinese text in characters and in pinyin romanization, followed by a figurative translation with extensive annotations in endnotes. I designed The Lyrical Lu Xun to help readers "approach" Lu Xun's poetry — the literal glosses and annotations are intended to help students read the poems themselves. David Hawkes did this in his book *A Little Primer of Tu Fu*, but he did not provide figurative translations, instead he ended up writing prose translations in paragraphs rather than in verse, which proved disappointing to some readers.

6. QUESTION: Do you think emphasizing rhyme and metre will distort the meaning and decrease the reader's understanding?

ANSWER: Not necessarily — this depends in part on the poem itself and in part on the skill of the translator. I find the readers with the least patience for this approach are people who think of themselves as contemporary poets in the US, who usually avoid rhyme as part of an aesthetic redefinition of modern poetry that was reached sometime after the Civil War. Their idea was that rhyme is at the same time predictable and grandiloquent, and hence not modern. But since I am a scholar of Chinese literature and not a contemporary American poet, I guess I can afford to take some aesthetic risks. Jonathan Chaves at Georgetown University agrees with this position. One of my American poet friends (Charles Belbin, now teaching English at City College of San Francisco) once said he thought I had allowed myself to become overly-influenced by having lived in China and had adopted Chinese ideas about how Chinese poetry should sound in English translation. Charles' implication was that if you are translating Chinese poetry into English, you need to give readers of English what they expect to see, not what Chinese readers want to see.

But I think in this particular instance another important factor to bear in mind is that Lu Xun wrote the majority of his classical-style poems in the 1930s, during the last five or six years of his life. It was a genre that he returned to after the new-style poetry written in the vernacular language had finally begun to make headway with the poetry of Zhu Xiang, Xu Zhimo, Zhu Ziqing, Wen Yiduo, etc. In a sense, Lu Xun was being archaistic in choosing to write this sort of classical-style verse in the ancient literary language and he was doing so for a variety of reasons, so I think that the archaistic feeling of the poems ought to be at least hinted at in the target language (English), hence the use of rhyme is justifiable here but not necessarily so in translating Du Fu or Bai Juyi, who were writing in the style of their own day. Bai Juyi in fact made an effort to use language so plain and simple that ill-educated or uneducated vendors in the marketplace could understand an oral recitation of his poetry. That's different from Lu Xun's style, which in addition to being written in the classical language, tonal and rhyme schemes, often employs symbolic and highly allusive language. Therefore, I would translate Lu Xun's classical-style verse using rhyme in English, but not necessarily Du Fu or Bai Juyi. And in The Subtle Revolution, my book on late-Qing / early Republican-era poets I did not employ rhyme in my translations because those poets were not being intentionally archaistic — they were standard during the late Qing.

7. QUESTION: What is the metre pattern that you used in translating the untitled poem (beginning Guanyu changye "Accustomed to long nights...") and Dao Yang Quan (In Memoriam for Yang Quan)?

ANSWER: Yang Xianyi once commented on my translations: "Ruguo gongwei ni yi ju, jiushi 'zi cheng feng ge'. He then said in English: "If I were to compliment you, I would say that you have created your own original style." He continued in English: "You do not imitate other people's verse or fall back on forms like 'heroic couplets,' which other translators tend to do."

I would conclude by saying that I am encouraged by the enthusiasm now being expressed for Lu Xun's poetry among both younger and older scholars in China and overseas and hope that, in some small way, my translations will add more fuel to the "subterranean fire" that Lu Xun once predicted would burst forth.

Remarkable changes have taken place in China since I first began reading Lu Xun. One cannot say his works have been without influence in some way on each and every one. At the same time, Lu Xun's name has been gaining in prominence and stature in the West. He himself summed it all up at the end of his short story Guxiang (*My Old Home*), observing: "Originally there were no roads across the earth, but when many people began to walk a certain way, paths were formed."

# 目录 | Contents

- **001** 别诸弟（三首）
  *Three Verses on Parting from My Brothers*
- **004** 莲蓬人
  *Lotus Seedpod People*
- **006** 庚子送灶即事
  *Feelings Upon Seeing off the Kitchen God in the Year 1901*
- **008** 祭书神文
  *An Offertory for the God of Books*
- **012** 别诸弟（三首）
  *Three Verses on Parting from My Brothers*
- **018** 无题（自题小像）
  *Untitled（Personally Inscribed on a Small Picture）*
- **020** 哀范君（三章）
  *Three Stanzas Mourning Fan Ainong*

| 024 | 替豆其伸冤
Redressing Grievances on Behalf of the Beanstalks |
|---|---|
| 026 | 吊卢骚
My Heartfelt Sympathies for Rousseau |
| 028 | 无题（题赠冯蕙熹）
Untitled (For Feng Huixi) |
| 030 | 赠邬其山
For Wu Qishan (Uchiyama Kanzo) |
| 032 | 附：无题（佛偈一首）
Appendix: Untitled (A Buddhist rhyme) |
| 034 | 送O.E.君携兰归国
For Mr. O.E. on the Occasion of his Return [to Japan] with [a Shipment of] Orchids |
| 036 | 无题（悼柔石）
Untitled (A Lament for Rou Shi) |
| 038 | 送日本歌人
For a Japanese Poet |
| 040 | 无题
Untitled |
| 042 | 湘灵歌
Ode to the Goddess of the Xiang River |

| 044 | 无题（二首） |
| --- | --- |
| | *Two Untitled Poems* |
| 048 | 送增田涉君归国 |
| | *For Masuda Wataru on the Occasion of His Return to Japan* |
| 050 | 南京民谣 |
| | *Lyrics for a Nanking Ditty* |
| 052 | 答客诮 |
| | *In Answer to a Gibe from a Guest* |
| 054 | 无题 |
| | *Untitled* |
| 056 | 偶成 |
| | *An Impromptu Composition* |
| 058 | 赠蓬子 |
| | *For Pengzi* |
| 060 | 一·二八战后作 |
| | *Written After the January Twenty-eighth Conflict* |
| 062 | 自嘲 |
| | *Laughing at My Own Predicament* |
| 064 | 教授杂咏（四首） |
| | *Desultory Versifying on Professors* |

| | |
|---|---|
| 068 | 所闻 |
| | *Hearsay* |
| 070 | 无题（赠滨之上、坪井）（二首） |
| | *Two Untitled Poems* |
| 074 | 无题 |
| | *Untitled* |
| 076 | 二十二年元旦 |
| | *New Year's Day in the Twenty-second Year of the Republic* |
| 078 | 赠画师 |
| | *For a Master Painter* |
| 080 | 学生和玉佛 |
| | *Students and Jade Buddhas* |
| 082 | 吊大学生 |
| | *Lamenting the College Students —— in the style of Cui Hao's "Yellow Crane Pavilion"* |
| 086 | 题《呐喊》 |
| | *Inscribed in a Copy of Outcry* |
| 088 | 题《彷徨》 |
| | *Inscribed in a Copy of Hesitation* |

| 090 | 悼杨铨
A Lament for Yang Quan

| 092 | 题三义塔
Inscription for the Stupa of the Three Fidelities

| 096 | 无题
Untitled

| 098 | 悼丁君
A Lament for Ms. Ding

| 100 | 赠人（二首）
Two Poems for a Friend

| 104 | 无题
Untitled

| 106 | 无题
Untitled

| 108 | 阻郁达夫移家杭州
Against Yu Dafu's Move to Hangzhou

| 112 | 报载患脑炎戏作
A Spoof on Newspaper Reports that I had Contracted Encephalitis

| 114 | 无题
Untitled

| 118 | 秋夜有感 |
| --- | --- |
| | *Feelings on an Autumn Night* |
| 120 | 题《芥子园画谱·三集》赠许广平 |
| | *Inscribed on Part III of Mustard-seed Garden, Illustrated Guide to the Art of Chinese Painting* |
| 124 | 亥年残秋偶作 |
| | *Composed on an Impulse in Late Autumn of 1935* |
| 127 | 鲁迅旧体诗注释和英译略述 |
| | [澳] 寇志明 著　黄乔生 译 |
| | *Jon Eugene von Kowallis　Huang Qiaosheng* |
| 157 | 编后记 |
| | *Editor's Notes* |

# 别诸弟（三首）

## 一

谋生无奈日奔驰，
有弟偏教各别离。
最是令人凄绝处，
孤檠长夜雨来时。

## 二

还家未久又离家，
日暮新愁分外加。
夹道万株杨柳树，
望中都化断肠花。

## 三

从来一别又经年，
万里长风送客船。
我有一言应记取，
文章得失不由天。

（1900年3月）

# Three Verses on Parting from My Brothers

March 1900

### I

Careers and plans leave no great choice
save dashing 'bout to meet the day...
Thus brothers were mine only to
forsake them both and go away.
What scene could make one feel the more
alone or sore disheartened
Than the length of night by one lone lamp
that coming rains now portend?

### II

Returned home but a while,
again I'm leaving home;
And now the dusk adds extra bite
to sadness where I roam.

Ten thousand weeping willow trees line the road
on which I have departed
Gazing deep therein, I see them change
to flowers of the brokenhearted.

### III

As before, once parted,
another year must pass.
A wind ten thousand li in length
sends off the traveler's craft.
One word to leave with you I have,
and may you mark it well:
'Tis hardly all in "talent"
if at writing you'd excel.

# 莲 蓬 人

芰裳荇带处仙乡,
风定犹闻碧玉香。
鹭影不来秋瑟瑟,
苇花伴宿露瀼瀼。
扫除腻粉呈风骨,
褪却红衣学淡妆。
好向濂溪称净植,
莫随残叶堕寒塘!

(1900年秋)

# Lotus Seedpod People

### Autumn 1900

In water-caltrop raiment clad, with belt of floating-heart,
you dwell in faerie wonderlands.
Such lush jade-green, your perfumed hue —
tho' wind may cease, its fragrance yet expands.
Egrets' reflections grace this pond no more,
only the autumn wind's soughing, a soughing so glum.
Alone, but for the rush flower,
you bear the nocturne wake
and await the heavy dew that with the morn will come.
With greasy make-up swept away,
true character takes form!
Red garments loud, stripped off display
strength of a subtler norm!
Live up to what Lianxi said:
stand up "so straight and tall."
Follow not the withered leaves
in chilly ponds to fall!

## 庚子送灶即事

只鸡胶牙糖，
典衣供瓣香。
家中无长物，
岂独少黄羊！

（1901年2月11日）

# Feelings Upon Seeing off the Kitchen God in the Year 1901

February 11, 1901

A chicken and the "Teeth Gluing Sweet" ...
Clothing pawned for incense that we mete.
Our household, of every last thing depleted,
Still more than a yellow lamb has been deleted!

# 祭书神文

上章困敦之岁，贾子祭诗之夕，会稽戛剑生等谨以寒泉冷华，祀书神长恩，而缀之以俚词曰：

今之夕兮除夕，香焰氤氲兮烛焰赤。钱神醉兮钱奴忙，君独何为兮守残籍？华筵开兮腊酒香，更点点兮夜长。人喧呼兮入醉乡，谁荐君兮一觞。绝交阿堵兮尚剩残书，把酒大呼兮君临我居。緗旗兮芸舆，挈脉望兮驾蠹鱼。寒泉兮菊菹，狂诵《离骚》兮为君娱。君之来兮毋除除，君友漆妃兮管城侯。向笔海而啸傲兮，倚文冢以淹留。不妨导脉望而登仙兮，引蠹鱼之来游。俗丁伧父兮为君仇，勿使履阈兮增君忧。若勿听兮止以吴钩，示之《丘》《索》兮棘其喉。令管城脱颖以出兮，使彼惙惙以心愁。宁召书癖兮来诗囚，君为我守兮乐未休。他年芹茂而樨香兮，购异籍以相酬。

（1901年2月18日）

# An Offertory for the God of Books

February 18, 1901

In the lunar year gengzi (1901), on the very eve when, in days of yore, the poet Jia Dao (779-843) annually brought forth the fruits of his literary labors — his poems — and offered them up to the God of Books, I, Jiajian Sheng of Kuaiji County [in the modern Shaoxing city] reverently bring forth "chilled springwater" [i.e. wine] and cold flowery [fruits] for Chang En, God of Books, garnishing them with this unpolished verse:

This evening, the Eve of the New Year
clouds of smoke bellow from incense glow,
red burn the candles' flames.
The God of Wealth is drunk,
for the slaves of money now busy themselves.
Why doest Thou stand alone
Keeping guard over battered tomes?
A sumptuous feast is in the offering
with fragrant New Year's wine.

Toll after toll of the night watchman's bell,

on drags the night long.

While all the others clamor,

falling into the land of drunkenness,

Who remains to offer Thee

even one goblet?

I am severing relations with that "thing" [money],

yet will have my worn volumes still!

Lifting high my wine, in toast I cry

for Thou approachest my domicile.

In a flurry of silken banners, riding a carriage

of rue drawn by a team of silverfish

Thou comest leading Mai Wang,

renowned faerie bookworm.

I wait with cold spring-water wine,

and chrysanthemum-garnished delights;

With wild abandon chant forth verses of the Li Sao,

that these might delight Thee.

Tarry not in Thy coming,

O Friend of the Concubine of Black

and that Once-Ennobled Pen!

Sing out in exultation o'er the sea of writing brushes!

I bid thee relax and linger longer —

Lean on the graves of writings [dug by the loved ones of letters].

Why not lead Mai Wang in a climb to faerieland,

bringing silverfish to come and romp about.

Yokel Dolt and Old Man Simpleton are Thine enemies!
Permit not their likes to darken Thy doorstep dine,
as such could tarnish Thy name.
Should they pay no heed,
Stop them with a curved Wu dagger!
Show them ancient classics on divination and the Nine Regions of old,
for when they attempt to intone the works of high antiquity,
the very words shall pierce their throats.
Remove the cap from a pen, that the writing tip be revealed
a sight disquieting to their ilk!
I would summon to me book addicts
and men imprisoned by the love of verse!
Guide well the literary ventures of this, Thy servant
and I promise Thee unceasing bliss.
Should, in the coming year, the watercress flourish
and the cassia flower give forth its fragrance,
Rare volumes shall I purchase and offer
in return for Thine indulgence!

# 别诸弟（三首）

## 一

梦魂常向故乡驰，
始信人间苦别离。
夜半倚床忆诸弟，
残灯如豆月明时。

## 二

日暮舟停老圃家，
棘篱绕屋树交加。
怅然回忆家乡乐，
抱瓮何时共养花？

## 三

春风容易送韶年，
一棹烟波夜驶船。
何事脊令偏傲我，
时随帆顶过长天！

仲弟次予去春留别元韵三章,即以送别,并索和。予每把笔,辄黯然而止。越十余日,客窗偶暇;潦草成句,即邮寄之。嗟乎!登楼陨涕,英雄未必忘家;执手消魂,兄弟竟居异地!深秋明月,照游子而更明;寒夜怨笳,遇羁人而增怨。此情此景,盖未有不悄然以悲者矣。

辛丑仲春戛剑生拟删草

(1901年3、4月)

# Three Verses on Parting from My Brothers

March or April 1901

I

My soul takes wing so oft in dream
to fly home whence I came,
And hence I've learnt that in this life
parting is the bitt'rest pain.
As thoughts turn towards my brothers dear
I toss and turn well nigh midnight.
The lampwick's flame flickers bean-sized —
about to expire 'mid bright moonlight.

II

At sunset our boat moors
by an old planter's house.
'Round his hut, a thorn fence —
above, intertwine boughs.

Crestfallen, I think back
on the old days at home,
Wondering when again I shall carry
a watering-crock of my own.

## III

Youth is seen-off easily
by spring breezes in their constant flight
O'er the misty waves we row,
navigating our boat by night.
Wherefore doth the wagtail
flaunt himself at me,
Sweeping by our mast-tip
'cross the sky so free?

*My middle brother [Zhou Zuoren] composed three poems in the same rhyme that I had used for my original "Three Verses on Parting from My Brothers" [written in February of 1900] and presented these to me on my recent departure [this year]. Thereupon he requested I compose an additional three poems according to the rhyme scheme in answer to his set. Each time I took up my pen to write verses in reply I was overcome by gloom and had to stop without setting anything down. After ten or more days had passed I chanced upon a bit of spare time and thereupon scratched out these verses, mailing them to him. Alas! I climbed atop a storied building and gazed off toward my home town through tears. Gallant heroes too, get home-*

*sick! Thoughts of grasping each other's hands at parting melt me with sorrow. We are truly living apart now! Late in autumn when the moon is bright, it seems especially radiant when shining on travelers and those far from home. On these cold nights the effect of the sound of a mournful jia [reed flute] is increased if the listener happens to be living in strange parts. With feelings and circumstances such as mine, there has probably never been anyone who could keep from becoming despondent due to the sorrows [of separation].*

绍兴水乡

# 无 题

(自题小像)

灵台无计逃神矢,
风雨如磐暗故园。
寄意寒星荃不察,
我以我血荐轩辕。

(1903年春夏)

# Untitled

(Personally Inscribed on a Small Picture)

Spring or Summer 1903

The Spirit Tower holds no plan
to dodge the arrows of gods or man;
These storms that strike like rocks a-fall
enshroud our land in their darkening pall.
A cold star might convey men's will,
but the Fragrant One lacks judgment still;
So I shall offer my blood up for
Xuan Yuan, our progenitor.

# 哀范君（三章）

## 一

风雨飘摇日，
余怀范爱农。
华颠萎寥落，
白眼看鸡虫。
世味秋荼苦，
人间直道穷。
奈何三月别，
竟尔失畸躬！

## 二

海草国门碧，
多年老异乡。
狐狸方去穴，
桃偶已登场。
故里寒云恶，
炎天凛夜长。

独沉清泠水,
能否涤愁肠?

## 三

把酒论当世,
先生小酒人。
大圜犹茗艼,
微醉自沉沦。
此别成终古,
从兹绝绪言。
故人云散尽,
我亦等轻尘!

(1912年7月)

# Three Stanzas Mourning Fan Ainong

July, 1912

### I

'Mid whirling wind and rain this day,
My memories of Ainong stay.
With thinning, dry, and graying hair
How his eyes would roll at the scrappers for fare!
His gorge rose at men's worldly lust —
What gain's in store for those who're just?
Three months away, at such a cost —
This uncouth friend I've truly lost.

### II

Its green our home-shore grass regained,
Each year that we abroad remained.
The foxes had just left their lairs,
When peach-wood puppets took stage chairs.

Cold clouds engulfing home bade ill;
Sultry summer had a long night's chill.
In that limpid river you sank alone to depart —
Could its waters cleanse your forlorn heart?

## III

Goblet in hand, you held forth on the day;
To a bit of drinking, often gave way.
Sure 'twas drink the whole world did confound,
That alone, slightly drunk,
you could sink and then drown.
This time our parting will be forever,
What you left unsaid, I'll know now never.
Old friends finished like a cloud by a gust,
Thus what am I but some specks of light dust!

## 替豆萁伸冤

煮豆燃豆萁,
萁在釜下泣。
我烬你熟了,
正好办教席。

（1925年6月5日）

# Redressing Grievances on Behalf of the Beanstalks

### June 5, 1925

To cook the beans they burn bean vine
Beneath the cauldron beanstalks whine.
"Your career advanced, when to ash we turned,
Have your banquets now, for which we burned!"

# 吊卢骚

脱帽怀铅出，
先生盖代穷。
头颅行万里，
失计造儿童。

（1928年4月10日）

# My Heartfelt Sympathies for Rousseau

April 10, 1928

Cap removed [in forced obeisance],
you took your quill and left;
In your day, sir, was
no other so hard pressed.
Since your head, to China now,
this lengthy journey has to make;
A setback indeed have the ideals of É mile
[by Liang] been forced to take.

# 无 题

(题赠冯蕙熹)

杀人有将,
救人为医。
杀了大半,
救其孑遗。
小补之哉,
呜呼噫嘻!

(1930年9月1日)

# Untitled

(For Feng Huixi)

September 1, 1930

To kill people we have generals,
Those who save people are the doctors.
When the greater portion are slain,
To be healed, few remain —
Small help to things awry.
I can but weep and cry!

# 赠邬其山

廿年居上海，
每日见中华。
有病不求药，
无聊才读书。
一阔脸就变，
所砍头渐多。
忽而又下野，
南无阿弥陀。

（1931年2、3月）

# For Wu Qishan (Uchiyama Kanzo)

### February or March 1931

Twenty years in Shanghai did you stay,
Glimpsing China's splendors every day:
Afflictions for which medicine's not sought,
And study just as boredom's afterthought;
A volte-face when fortune comes their way —
Decapitations increase by the day.
Then suddenly they're on the outs again,
"Let's trust the Amitabha Lord, Amen!"

# 附：无题（佛偈一首）

放下屠刀，
立地成佛。
放下佛经，
立地杀人。

这首佛偈是写给日本传教士清水安三（1891—1988）的，参见黄乔生《朝花夕拾又思君——清水安三藏鲁迅手书佛偈》，载《海内与海外》2016年第2期。

# Appendix: Untitled (A Buddhist rhyme)

> Laying down their butcher knives,
> Suddenly transformed into Buddhas.
> They again lay down the sutras,
> Suddenly to resume their murders.

*This Buddhist rhyme was written by Lu Xun in a calligraphic style for the Japanese Christian missionary Shimizu Yasuzo (1891—1988), with whom he was acquainted over a period of years. In terms of content, it bears comparison with his poem for Uchiyama Kanzo. See Huang Qiaosheng: Dawn Blossom Plucked by Dusk: A Buddhist Rhyme in Lu Xun's Handwriting in the collection of Shimizu Yasuzo. Beijing, Home and Overseas, No.2, 2016.*

# 送O.E.君携兰归国

椒焚桂折佳人老,
独托幽岩展素心。
岂惜芳馨遗远者,
故乡如醉有荆榛。

(1931年2月12日)

# For Mr. O.E. on the Occasion of his Return [to Japan] with [a Shipment of] Orchids

### February 12, 1931

Pepper plant put to flame and cassia flower broken,
comely men grow old.
Only consigned to secluded crags
can pure hearts unfold.
How can we feel reluctant to give
this fragrant cargo to one from afar,
When our own old home, as if drunk,
has its brambles and thorns [to prick and scar!]

# 无 题

（悼柔石）

惯于长夜过春时，
挈妇将雏鬓有丝。
梦里依稀慈母泪，
城头变幻大王旗。
忍看朋辈成新鬼，
怒向刀丛觅小诗。
吟罢低眉无写处，
月光如水照缁衣。

（1931年2月末）

# Untitled

(A Lament for Rou Shi)

late February 1931

To long and sleepless night I've grown
accustomed in the spring;
Fled with a wife and babe in arms,
my temples are graying.
'Mid dream there comes an image faint
a loving mother's tear;
On city walls the overlords'
e'er-changing banners rear.
I can but stand by looking on
as friends become new ghosts,
In anger face bayonet thickets
and search for verse ripostes.
The poem intoned, my gaze turns low
one cannot write such down.
Moonlight shimmers with watery sheen
upon my jet-black gown.

## 送日本歌人

春江好景依然在，
远国征人此际行。
莫向遥天望歌舞，
西游演了是封神。

（1931年3月5日）

# For a Japanese Poet

March 5, 1931

Spring River's fine scenery is,
as always, grand;
Voyager, departing now,
to his far-off land.
Gaze not at the distant sky,
recalling song and dance.
For Journey to the West has run,
now... Ennobled Gods' Romance.

# 无 题

大野多钩棘,
长天列战云。
几家春袅袅,
万籁静愔愔。
下土唯秦醉,
中流辍越吟。
风波一浩荡,
花树已萧森。

（1931年3月5日）

# Untitled

March 5, 1931

So vast a countryside
the barbed bramble enflanks,
Across the lengths of heaven
warclouds drawn up in ranks.
Of spring's gentle breezes
few families enjoy their fill,
Ten thousand sounding things
hushed with an ominous still.
This lower world fell to Qin,
all of Heaven's caprice,
And now amidst the torrent's course
our bold Yue songs cease.
When a seething storm
bursts forth its turbulence:
Trees are left barren —
flowers lose their scents.

## 湘灵歌

昔闻湘水碧如染,
今闻湘水胭脂痕。
湘灵妆成照湘水,
皎如皓月窥彤云。
高丘寂寞竦中夜,
芳荃零落无余春。
鼓完瑶瑟人不闻,
太平成象盈秋门。

(1931年3月5日)

# Ode to the Goddess of the Xiang River

March 5, 1931

Once ran the Xiang, 'twas said of old,
bluer than indigo,
Yet rouge streamers now add new hue
to her former cyan flow.
The Xiang's surface, made mirror to
the Goddess' made-up face,
Shines glowing white like a pale moon
that crimson clouds encase.
Solitary stillness on this lofty hill —
fear and trembling deep in night.
Fragrant grasses wither and fall —
the passing spring gains no respite.
The inlayed zither's final notes
are heard by none of late,
As the trappings of a wondrous peace
glut the Autumnal Gate.

# 无题(二首)

## 一

大江日夜向东流,
聚义英雄又远游。
六代绮罗成旧梦,
石头城上月如钩。

## 二

雨花台边埋断戟,
莫愁湖里余微波。
所思美人不可见,
归忆江天发浩歌。

(1931年6月14日)

# Two Untitled Poems

### June 14, 1931

### I

Eastward by night and day,
the Great River flows on;
Our righteous heroes meet,
then sojourn forth anon.
Six Dynasties' silk fineries
become but bygone dreams.
Above the City of the Stone
a hook-like moon now gleams.

### II

By Raining Flowers Terrace nigh
the broken halberds buried lie;
Sorrow-not Lake is yet astir
with ripplets churning off her shore.

The noble beauties on my mind,
one can search for, but never find.
Recalling, o'er the river's sky,
in mighty song my sorrows fly.

大江日夜向東流,聚沫狂熊又遠遊。六代綺羅成舊夢,石頭城上月如鉤。

宮崎先生屬

魯迅

无题

# 送增田涉君归国

扶桑正是秋光好,
枫叶如丹照嫩寒。
却折垂杨送归客,
心随东棹忆华年。

（1931年12月2日）

# For Masuda Wataru on the Occasion of His Return to Japan

December 2, 1931

> Your Isle of Sacred Trees displays
> an autumn landscape fine these days;
> And maple leaves of crimson hue,
> with chill, produce a redder view.
> Yet to see you off, right here I stand,
> a broken willow branch in hand;
> My mind's eye follows your east-bound oars
> back to a youth spent on those shores.

## 南京民谣

大家去谒陵,
强盗装正经。
静默五分钟,
各自想拳经。

(1931年12月25日)

# Lyrics for a Nanking Ditty

December 25, 1931

On the Sun Mausoleum's lofty stairs,
Robbers pay homage with solemn airs:
In a ten-minute silence, side by side there,
Each plots his next move when the struggles flare.

# 答客诮

无情未必真豪杰,
怜子如何不丈夫。
知否兴风狂啸者,
回眸时看小於菟。

(1931年末或1932年初)

# In Answer to a Gibe from a Guest

*late 1931 or early 1932*

Must a true he-man
be unfeeling and cold?
Cannot a doting father
be a hero untold?
Know you not that tigers,
whose mighty roar winds send,
Often take a backward glance
for their cubs to fend.

# 无 题

血沃中原肥劲草，
寒凝大地发春华。
英雄多故谋夫病，
泪洒崇陵噪暮鸦。

（1932年1月23日）

# Untitled

January 23, 1932

Blood enriches the Central Plain,
giving hardy grasses fertile earth;
Across a vast and frozen land
flowers of spring come bursting forth.
Afflictions plague our "heroes" now,
as aides-de-camp have taken ill;
That revered tomb is drenched with tears —
by eventide crows clamor still.

# 偶 成

文章如土欲何之,
翘首东云惹梦思。
所恨芳林寥落甚,
春兰秋菊不同时。

（1932年3月31日）

# An Impromptu Composition

### March 31, 1932

Writings worth their weight in dirt,
wither can one go?
Head raised toward the eastern clouds,
dreams and thoughts now flow...
A woeful sight this fragrant grove,
its florae sparse and few;
The autumn mum can share no days
with orchids that spring grew.

# 赠蓬子

蓦地飞仙降碧空，
云车双辆挈灵童。
可怜蓬子非天子，
逃去逃来吸北风。

（1932年3月31日）

# For Pengzi

March 31, 1932

Abruptly bounds a flying faerie
down from out of the clear blue;
In a pair of cloud chariots,
leading her wonder child too.
A pity that Pengzi
was not her Tianzi;
Fleeing back and forth to wit's end,
her only sustenance the north wind.

## 一·二八战后作

战云暂敛残春在，
重炮清歌两寂然。
我亦无诗送归棹，
但从心底祝平安。

（1932年7月11日）

# Written After the January Twenty-eighth Conflict

### July 11, 1932

The clouds of war withdrawn a while,
snatches of spring remain;
Those heavy guns and arias —
silence befalls the twain.
Nor do I have a single verse
to offer as we part,
I can but wish you peace
from the bottom of my heart.

# 自　嘲

运交华盖欲何求，
未敢翻身已碰头。
破帽遮颜过闹市，
漏船载酒泛中流。
横眉冷对千夫指，
俯首甘为孺子牛。
躲进小楼成一统，
管他冬夏与春秋。

（1932年10月12日）

# Laughing at My Own Predicament

### October 12, 1932

What's to be done under ill-boding stars
with such a change of luck,
Before I'd even dared rise up,
my head already struck!
A worn-out hat to cover my face,
I cross the busy market place;
In a leaky boat loaded with wine,
'mid torrent float as though supine.
Eyes askance, I cast a cold glance
at the thousand pointing fingers;
But bowing my head, I gladly agree,
an ox for the children to be.
In a little garret hidden away,
I make my bid at unité;
Of outside climes, why care at all —
be it winter, summer, spring or fall.

# 教授杂咏（四首）

一

作法不自毙，
悠然过四十。
何妨赌肥头，
抵挡辩证法。

二

可怜织女星，
化为马郎妇。
乌鹊疑不来，
迢迢牛奶路。

三

世界有文学，
少女多丰臀。

鸡汤代猪肉,
北新遂掩门。

### 四

名人选小说,
入线云有限。
虽有望远镜,
无奈近视眼。

(1932年12月29日)

# Desultory Versifying on Professors

December 29, 1932

I

You create "laws"
you don't live by:
Having eased past forty,
you still don't die.
Why not try wagering your
own fat head
Dialectics in its tracks
to stop dead.

II

How piteous the star
known as the Weaving Maid,
Into a horse-groom's bride
she's been transmogrified.

Dismayed, the magpies
will ne'er bestride
A "Cow's Milk Road"
so vast and wide.

### III

The world
has its literature,
And girlies' voluptuous
derrieres' allure.
With chicken soup galore,
partake of pork no more;
'Twas thus Bei Xin Bookstore
thought best to close its door.

### IV

Big-name editor compiles
a short story anthology;
Those who can make the grade, you claim,
are a select company.
Though you have a spyglass
for looking all around,
By this sort of nearsight,
you'll be forever bound!

## 所　闻

华灯照宴敞豪门，
娇女严装侍玉樽。
忽忆情亲焦土下，
佯看罗袜掩啼痕。

（1932年12月31日）

# Hearsay

December 31, 1932

Colorful lanterns brighten the feast
seen through a gaping gate;
A tender girl, precise in dress,
serves the jade-goblet fête.
Her mind turns toward the scorched-earth grave
where lie those to her dear;
Feigning to adjust her silken hose,
she hides the tracks of tear.

# 无题（二首）

（赠滨之上、坪井）

一

故乡黯黯锁玄云，
遥夜迢迢隔上春。
岁暮何堪再惆怅，
且持卮酒吃河豚。

二

皓齿吴娃唱柳枝，
酒阑人静暮春时。
无端旧梦驱残醉，
独对灯阴忆子规。

（1932年12月31日）

# Two Untitled Poems

December 31, 1932

### I (For Hamanoue)

My old home locked in murky clouds,
so dark, yet ever darkening;
On, drag on, unending night
that hinders the coming spring.
At dusk of the year, why draw more near
the breaking point in anguish?
Let us lift, for the time, a goblet of wine
and partake of a globefish.

### II (For Tsuboi)

A Jiangsu doll croons "Willow Branches"
through teeth a lustrous white;
Voices still, as the wine runs low,
spring's dusk draws toward its night.

A tipsy mood now chased away,
as dreams lurch from the past;
Alone, recall a cuckoo's form
'mid shadows the lamp's cast.

故乡黯黯锁玄云，屡夜屏，
偏上春岁暮行堪再惆怅，
且持卮酒吿雲河豚

无题

# 无 题

洞庭木落楚天高,
眉黛猩红浣战袍。
泽畔有人吟不得,
秋波渺渺失离骚。

(1932年12月31日)

# Untitled

### December 31, 1932

Lake Dongting's trees have shed their leaves
'neath a towering Chu sky;
Traces of kohl and blood-red stains
brave warriors' robes belie.
Alack, that poets pace the shores
with verses they can ne'er decry...
Today our Li Sao disappears
'mid autumn waves that billow high.

## 二十二年元旦

云封高岫护将军,
霆击寒村灭下民。
到底不如租界好,
打牌声里又新春。

(1933年1月26日)

# New Year's Day in the Twenty-second Year of the Republic

January 26, 1933

A mist-enveloped lofty peak
shelters our Generalissimo.
Thunderbolts striking villages bleak
exterminate the common and low.
A far cry better the lifestyle
enjoyed in the Foreign Concession.
Amid the clacking of mahjong pieces,
a new spring is upon us again.

## 赠 画 师

风生白下千林暗,
雾塞苍天百卉殚。
愿乞画家新意匠,
只研朱墨作春山。

（1933年1月26日）

# For a Master Painter

January 26, 1933

A wind arose from old Nanking
that darkens a thousand groves;
Fog blocks out the azure sky,
and flowers wilt in droves.
I beseech thee, painter, to show forth
thy novel artistry:
Grind but crimson ink to paint spring peaks —
to this wilt thou agree?

## 学生和玉佛

寂寞空城在，
仓皇古董迁。
头儿夸大口，
面子靠中坚。
惊扰讵云妄，
奔逃只自怜。
所嗟非玉佛，
不值一文钱。

（1933年1月30日）

# Students and Jade Buddhas

### January 30, 1933

Forlorn, the empty city stands,
in a flurry, her ancient relics removed.
For face-saving, our big-talking "heads",
are to "the backbone of society" behooved,
Alarm in times like these — wherefore deem it panic?
they flee, self-preservation bent.
Not born Jade Buddhas, they lament
their lives are nary worth a cent.

## 吊大学生

阔人已骑文化去，
此地空余文化城。
文化一去不复返，
古城千载冷清清。
专车队队前门站，
晦气重重大学生。
日薄榆关何处抗，
烟花场上没人惊。

（1933年1月31日）

# Lamenting the College Students
—— in the style of Cui Hao's "Yellow Crane Pavilion"

January 31, 1933

Gone the grandees, who already
rode off on the objets d'art of our culture.
Empty, this place from whence they took flight,
save for the name "City of Culture."
Those objets d'art, once gone,
shall ne'er return again;
Tho' the ancient city, for a thousand years
in sullen emptiness remain.
Before Qianmen Station
queue lines of express trains;
But for our college students,
luck has run out.
Whither our resistance when at Yu Pass

the Rising Sun they fly?
Yet those in the brothels still demand:
"What's all this hue and cry!"

鲁迅正面照

# 题《呐喊》

弄文罹文网,
抗世违世情。
积毁可销骨,
空留纸上声。

(1933年3月2日)

# Inscribed in a Copy of *Outcry*

### March 2, 1933

Dallying with writings,
one gets caught in a written net;
Resisting the times,
runs afoul of worldly sentiment.
Slander, when built up,
can dissolve the very bone:
I leave behind naught
but words on paper strown.

## 题《彷徨》

寂寞新文苑,
平安旧战场。
两间余一卒,
荷戟独彷徨。

（1933年3月2日）

# Inscribed in a Copy of *Hesitation*

March 2, 1933

Our new literary garden
in forlorn silence placed,
The old battlegrounds,
with tranquil calm are graced.
Somewhere 'twixt the two,
a lone foot-soldier standing by,
Shoulders his halberd,
wandering the earth and sky.

# 悼杨铨

岂有豪情似旧时，
花开花落两由之。
何期泪洒江南雨，
又为斯民哭健儿。

（1933年6月20日）

# A Lament for Yang Quan

June 20, 1933

Gone, I thought, impassioned moods
like those of long ago:
Flowers blossomed, flowers fell —
and of their own did so.
That tears would fall 'mid Southern rain
— how was I then to know
Our people's loss of a dauntless son
could plunge me again to woe?

# 题三义塔

三义塔者,中国上海闸北三义里遗鸠埋骨之塔也,在日本,农人共建之。

奔霆飞焰歼人子,
败井颓垣剩饿鸠。
偶值大心离火宅,
终遗高塔念瀛洲。
精禽梦觉仍衔石,
斗士诚坚共抗流。
度尽劫波兄弟在,
相逢一笑泯恩仇。

西村博士于上海战后得丧家之鸠,持归养之;初亦相安,而终化去。建塔以藏,且征题咏,率成一律,聊答遐情云尔。一九三三年六月二十一日鲁迅并记。

# Inscription for the Stupa of the Three Fidelities

June 21, 1933

*The Stupa of the Three Fidelities was built with the help of peasants in Japan; here the remains of a dove from Three Fidelities Lane in the Zhabei section of Shanghai, China are interred.*

Dashing thunder and flying flame
leave mortal men slain;
'Mid crumbling walls and caved-in wells
a hungry dove remains.
By chance he meets a kindly heart
and leaves the fiery dwelling;
In old Nippon a lofty tomb
commemorates our starveling.
Were he to wake as though from dream,
the dove's shade would carry pebbles;
And stand with comrades resolute —

'gainst tide and flood as rebels.
We brothers will yet see the day
when stormy surges all abate;
On reuniting, with one smile,
we'll wash away the hate.

*Dr. Nishimura found a homeless dove after the fighting in Shanghai, which he then took back to Japan with him to raise. At first it got on well but later passed away, so a stupa was erected in which to bury the dove. Asked to supply a verse for the stupa, I scratched out this poem in response to these sentiments from afar. June 21, 1933. Lu Xun.*

奔霆飞熛歼豗族，
人子败井颓垣。
腾饿鸠偶值
大心离大宅，
终遣高塔念
瀛洲精禽
梦觉仍御石
斗士诚坚共抗
流度壶劫波
兄弟在相逢
一笑泯恩雠

题三义塔

# 无　题

禹域多飞将,
蜗庐剩逸民。
夜邀潭底影,
玄酒颂皇仁。

（1933年6月28日）

# Untitled

### June 28, 1933

O'er the Realm of Yu,
many Flying Generals zoom.
Yet in some snail-shell down below,
a recluse has eluded doom.
By night he invites
his reflection in a pool
To toast with heaven's wine The Emperor's merciful rule.

# 悼丁君

如磐夜气压重楼,
剪柳春风导九秋。
瑶瑟凝尘清怨绝,
可怜无女耀高丘。

（1933年6月28日）

# A Lament for Ms. Ding

June 28, 1933

On storied buildings endless night
weighs down like flagstones overhead;
Spring's breeze that once shaped willow trees
to Autumn's Ninety Days has led.
The inlayed zither now dust-choked,
its clear and poignant music stops;
Alack that we're without the maid
who lit up lonely mountain tops!

# 赠人（二首）

## 一

明眸越女罢晨妆，
荇水荷风是旧乡。
唱尽新词欢不见，
旱云如火扑晴江。

## 二

秦女端容理玉筝，
梁尘踊跃夜风轻。
须臾响急冰弦绝，
但见奔星劲有声。

（1933年7月21日）

# Two Poems for a Friend

### July 21, 1933

### I

Bright-eyed Zhejiang girl,
her morning toilet made,
From a river village where wind-swept lotus
and water plants pervade.
The new songs sung,
her lover nowhere to be found;
O'er that now parched river
fiery drought clouds bound.

### II

By a Shaanxi girl of dignified face,
an ornamented zither played;
Rafter dust undulating in cadence...
the night wind, by music allayed.
In an instant switch to a frantic pitch

an ice-white string snaps outright;
Lo, behold the sound
of a falling star in its might.

五十三岁生辰照。1933年9月13日摄于上海

# 无 题

一枝清采妥湘灵,
九畹贞风慰独醒。
无奈终输萧艾密,
却成迁客播芳馨。

(1933年11月27日)

# Untitled

November 27, 1933

The Xiang goddess derives comfort
from an orchid pure;
'Tis but this wide-spread noble scent
that makes the loner sure.
Unable to stave off at last
these weeds, encroachment-bent;
In exile one can wander yet,
and spread the fragrant scent.

# 无 题

烟水寻常事,
荒村一钓徒。
深宵沉醉起,
无处觅菰蒲。

（1933年秋）

# Untitled

Autumn of 1933

Mist-shrouded waters
are the normal lot:
For a lone fisher
by deserted hamlet —
Deep in night,
arising drunken yet,
Reed and rush
are nowhere to be sought.

# 阻郁达夫移家杭州

钱王登假仍如在,
伍相随波不可寻。
平楚日和憎健翮,
小山香满蔽高岑。
坟坛冷落将军岳,
梅鹤凄凉处士林。
何似举家游旷远,
风波浩荡足行吟。

(1933年12月30日)

# Against Yu Dafu's Move to Hangzhou

### December 30, 1933

Long ago did tyrant Qian from this mortal world ascend,
[but today in old Hangzhou], it's as if he'll never go.
Wronged Prime Minister Wu Zixu,
[once the god of the tidal bore],
now drifts aimlessly with the wave, his body to be
sought no more.
Manicured trees, warm sun and balmy climes
suit not stout birds of hardy plume;
A spring peak, by flowers covered,
can but a hill's stature assume.
Forlorn and cold are the altar and tomb
of renowned general Yue Fei;
Hermit Lin's plum grove and crane pavilion
now in sorrowful disarray.
What are those things when your whole family

could traverse the far and wide?
See storm and sea in society —
inspired, you'd chant and stride.

三十日晴上午诗题无信 诗句上里（明年一月夕）二年五角 于戊为贽定

寿刀幅一律云 谈王水逝何处在 泛相随 烧不了 寻平楚日初惺

健翮小山香满嶽 高岑境壇 吟荷物军岳梅鹤凄凉画士

林行似华家游瘦远 风烟浩荡是行吟 又为芹振球书一幅云

烟小争家事无邪 一钓沧波自吹 辞起无妻爱荒甫 晚浮小

峰信寻纳税示二百 付去行渡洲争骂五干 纸藤之生表为两要义

梁珊诊

阻郁达夫移家杭州

## 报载患脑炎戏作

横眉岂夺蛾眉冶,
不料仍违众女心。
诅咒而今翻异样,
无如臣脑故如冰。

（1934年3月15日）

# A Spoof on Newspaper Reports that I had Contracted Encephalitis

### March 15, 1934

Could fierce brows for flattery e'er displace
their moth-like eyebrows and seductive face?
Who would have thought I'd provoked their ire,
kindling damsels' hearts with jealous fire?
They'd called down curses upon my head,
but this one's different from past ones spread.
'Twas of no avail, this malicious vice,
for my humble brain is as cool as ice.

# 无 题

万家墨面没蒿莱,
敢有歌吟动地哀。
心事浩茫连广宇,
于无声处听惊雷。

(1934年5月30日)

# Untitled

May 30, 1934

The dark and haggard faces of a countless host
are sunken in the bushes, living still, at most.
Yet who among us dares with song burst forth
a sorrow that could move the very earth?
Troubles boundless in my heart expand,
ranging the vastness of our land,
And in this place without a trace of sound,
I hear tremorous thunder raging 'round.

万家墨面没蒿莱，敢有歌吟动地哀。心事浩茫连广宇，于无声处听惊雷。

戊年初夏偶作以应

新房先生雅教

鲁迅

无题

摄于上海

## 秋夜有感

绮罗幕后送飞光,
柏栗丛边作道场。
望帝终教芳草变,
迷阳聊饰大田荒。
何来酪果供千佛,
难得莲花似六郎。
中夜鸡鸣风雨集,
起然烟卷觉新凉。

(1934年9月29日)

# Feelings on an Autumn Night

(September 29, 1934)

Amid gossamer silk-curtained pleasure,
fleeting time is whiled away as leisure;
While 'neath the chestnut and the cypress tree —
a requiem in all solemnity!
The cuckoo's plaintive cry that signals fall
has fragrant grasses wither, one and all;
And naught but thistle flowers are yet left
to decorate vast wastelands so bereft.
So whence shall come fruits fine enough indeed
to satisfy a host of Buddhas' need?
Nor can a lotus fair enough be found,
though to surpass Liu Lang 'twill not be bound.
This night the cock would rather crow than rest,
as wind and rain in storm together press;
Arising from my couch, a cigarette I light
and feel the chill of an early autumn night.

# 题《芥子园画谱·三集》赠许广平

　　此上海有正书局翻造本。其广告谓研究木刻十余年,始雕是书。实则兼用木版、石版、波黎版及人工着色,乃日本成法,非尽木刻也。广告夸耳!然原刻难得,翻本亦无胜于此者。因致一部,以赠广平,有诗为证:

　　　　十年携手共艰危,
　　　　以沫相濡亦可哀;
　　　　聊借画图怡倦眼,
　　　　此中甘苦两心知。

　　　　　　　　戊年冬十二月九日之夜,鲁迅记

# Inscribed on Part III of Mustard-seed Garden, Illustrated Guide to the Art of Chinese Painting

December 9, 1934

*This is a facsimile edition produced by Youzheng Book Company in Shanghai. The advertisements for the book claimed it was "produced only after ten years' research into woodblock printing techniques." Actually it was produced using the [modern] Japanese technique of combining woodblock, stone plate, collotype, and hand-tinting, so it is not entirely the product of [traditional Chinese polychromatic] woodblock printing. The advertising was simply exaggeration! Nevertheless, the original editions are rare, and among the reprinted versions, none is as good as this. For that reason I purchased a copy as a gift for Guangping and hereby dedicate it to her with a poem:*

For ten years, hand in hand,

together 'mid adversity;
Spewing saliva, we kept each other moist
as two fish aground might do.
Now take, a while, these painting books
and soothe your tired eyes;
The joys and sorrows of these years
were shared alone by you.

芥子園畫譜三集

此上海有正書局翻造本其廣告謂筆究木刻十餘年始雕成書實則兼用木版石版以黎版又人工著色乃日本成法非畫木刻也廣告誇耀然原刻難得翻本亦無勝于此者因致一部以贈廣平有詩為證

十年攜手共艱危以沫相濡亦可哀聊借畫圖怡倦眼此中甘苦兩心知

戊年冬十二月九日之夜 魯迅記

題《芥子園畫譜·三集》贈許廣平

## 亥年残秋偶作

曾惊秋肃临天下，
敢遣春温上笔端。
尘海苍茫沉百感，
金风萧瑟走千官。
老归大泽菰蒲尽，
梦坠空云齿发寒。
竦听荒鸡偏阒寂，
起看星斗正阑干。

（1935年12月5日）

# Composed on an Impulse in Late Autumn of 1935

December 5, 1935

Alarmed at autumn's grimness which
bore down upon the earth,
Would I have set my pen to write
how balmy spring is mirth?
Amid dust oceans' vastness sink
my passions hundred-fold;
To flee with soughing autumn wind —
officials all make bold!
To marshes in old age return,
where reed and rush are gone,
Chilled to the bone, when dreams that fall
through empty clouds are drawn.
I strain to hear a rooster crow —
in silence all stands by...
Arising, see the dipper sink,
and know the dawn is nigh.

曾惊秋肃临天下,敢遣春温上
笔端。尘海苍茫沉百感,金风
萧瑟走千官。老归大泽菰
蒲尽,梦坠空云齿发寒。竦
听荒鸡偏阒寂,起看星斗
正阑干

亥年残秋偶作朱庑
李市吾兄教正
鲁迅

# 鲁迅旧体诗注释和英译略述

[澳] 寇志明 著　黄乔生 译

自几年前《中国文学》的编辑第一次让我给黄新渠的译本《鲁迅的诗》(1979)写书评以来，学界又有几次将鲁迅（1881—1936）的古体诗译成英语的尝试，都以书的形式出版，并且有大量这方面的中文著作问世。从那时到现在，我在吸引其他学者去就其中的一些成果写评论方面的努力徒劳无功，又因为不愿对所有这些新著一一加以评析，因而《中国文学》的编辑就特地给了我一个机会，在讨论英文新译本的同时也讨论一些更有影响的中文旧著，并且讨论有关鲁迅旧体诗注释和翻译的一些一般性问题。这方面的著作我举主要的如下：

英文著作：

《鲁迅诗选》，吴钧陶译，上海外语教育出版社，1981年版，119页。

《鲁迅诗选》，詹纳尔译，北京，外文出版社，1982年版，160页。

《鲁迅诗全译》，陈颖译，坦佩，亚利桑那州立大学亚洲研究中心，1988年版，277页。

中文著作：

《鲁迅旧诗新诠》，司空无忌著，重庆文光书店，1947年。

《鲁迅旧诗笺注》，张向天（原名张秉新）著，广东人民出版社，1959/1962年版，两卷，213页。

《鲁迅旧诗笺注》，张向天著，香港，雅典美术印刷公司，1972—1973年版，656页。

《鲁迅诗歌注》，周振甫著，浙江人民出版社，1962年版，202页；修订版1980年版。

《鲁迅诗笺选集：附诗稿》，香港，文学研究社，1973年版，178页。

《鲁迅诗新解》，江天著，香港，文育出版社，出版日期不详。重印本名为《鲁迅诗注析》，姜添著，香港集思图书公司，1974年版。

《鲁迅旧诗浅说》，倪墨炎著，上海人民出版社1977年版。

《鲁迅旧诗集解》，张恩和著，天津人民出版社，1981年版，452页。

日文著作：

《鲁迅诗话》，高田淳著，东京，中央公论社，1971年版，256页。

鲁迅的"旧体诗"（中文是这么称呼的）大多数采用的是唐宋诗时代常见的式样（律诗和绝句），也有一些可以称作古体诗或骚体诗（受到楚辞风格的影响）。鲁迅与毛泽东（1893—1976）不一样,他写的诗大多有沉思、忧郁的风格,他不填词,而毛泽东则用词的形式来表达他那更激越的格调和更雄浑的情绪。

鲁迅的旧体诗现存的有64首,詹纳尔的译本并没有全部译出。吴钧陶的译本,虽然英文颇有毛病,却想竭力给出一个较全的选本,但却为了某些原因删掉了几首诗,尽管他收录了一些有争议的篇什如为丁玲和姚蓬子写的两首(姚蓬子是"四人帮"成员之一姚文元的父亲)。詹纳尔的译本,受到魏璐诗(Ruth Weiss)女士的赞赏——但这位女士自己承认,她在中国生活了五十年,却还不能阅读中文①——并且有已故的北京大学教授王瑶作序。这个译本是用颇为板滞的无韵体诗译出的,表面上看起来像是逐字逐句的直译。②尽管詹纳尔在书中告诉我们:"各诗的注释大大仰仗外文出版社编辑们的专业知识和大量有关这些诗的中文研究成果。这些参考借鉴我是乐于承认的……"(第25页)但他实际上并没有引出任何他据以诠释诗歌的资料来源。除了我本人那篇浅薄的硕士论文(1978),唯一一个将鲁迅旧体诗全部译为英文的尝试是陈颖(David Chen)的韵文译本,威廉·舒尔

---

① "最受欢迎的是1982年出版的《鲁迅诗选》,W.J.F. 詹纳尔译,……比尔·詹纳尔以前曾在这里——北京外文出版社——工作过,我发现他的中文知识很了不起。对我这样一个不能从原文阅读鲁迅的人来说……"见魏璐诗(Ruth F. Weiss):《鲁迅:一个跨时代的中国作家》(*Lu Xun: a Chinese Writer for All Times*),北京新世界出版社1985年版第293页。

② 詹纳尔的书开头好像要摆脱对译文的责任似的,警告说:"原文的简洁和平衡必然在翻译中大部分丧失掉,同样要牺牲词汇的文学和历史意义的运用(指用典),也就是几个世纪以来中国古典诗歌的特点之一。这些和谐不能在将之译成外国语言时留下来,只能在简短的评论(指注释)中部分地加以指明。因此需要请读者对鲁迅的这些诗的质量给予信任。"(第12页)

茨（William Schultz）在为该译本写的前言中介绍译者是俄亥俄州立大学的"中国现代文学研究专家"。

应该先申明一点，在翻译和解释鲁迅诗作中存在的一个问题是，许多更重要的诗作是用一种特别的多用隐喻的风格写出的，受到楚辞的影响；而从其所用的晦涩词语来看，又与晚唐诗人李商隐（813—858）的诗风相近。这么说固然好，有人也许会回答，但还是让我简单地把它们当作美的文学作品来看待吧。但这一点不是那么容易做到的，因为詹纳尔告诉我们："我试图只提示出读者必需的最低限度的信息就行了。我也试图避免注释过多，像在那些不愉快的年月里把鲁迅30年代所有的诗作的意义都描述成装腔作势的战斗姿态。"（第25—26页）当然，没有哪个人愿意为读一首诗而阅读很多材料，但20世纪30年代是一个在书报检查和暗杀方面形式颇为复杂的时代。①而且，按詹纳尔的逻辑，在"四人帮"被粉碎后中国出版物相对而言应该摆脱了"过度诠释"。然而从过去十几年的出版物来看，这也不一定是真实情况。

对于鲁迅旧体诗进行研究的中文专著，就我所见，最早的一本是二战刚刚结束时在重庆出版的一个小册子，但对我们这些对1949年以前的注释抱有较高期望的人来说，该书评释的武断和

---

① 詹纳尔译本的封底仍然坚持说："他（鲁迅）的晚年诗作（指30年代的诗）特别暴露了帝国主义和蒋介石政府的统治，表达了对劳苦大众的同情，赞扬了无产阶级的革命事业。"假设这些话是外文出版社的编辑拟定而非他本人所写，我们也不需要到更远处寻觅，在詹纳尔本人写的序言中也能看到30年代在上海的鲁迅被描述成："一个献身革命事业的职业作家。逮捕和暗杀的威胁追逐着他和与他接近的人。他多年来以他的杂文惹怒了很多人……"（第22页）还有："在对青年作家的悼念中，鲁迅的表达方式是直接的，带感情的，没有用什么典故，那首诗对读者们来说一看就能懂。"（第24页）

潦草浮面令人失望。

接下来的一本写于香港，1959年在广东印行，署名张向天，乃张秉新的化名。①这本单卷本的著作于1962年印行了第二版。随后在1972年和1973年在香港出了修订版，大大扩充，分为两卷，大体上可以算是该书的重写本了。就文本的评论来说，这本书是目前为止个人著述中最完备的一本著作。解说详细而易懂，但许多篇什的介绍文字过于冗长。张为每首诗做的白话释文有时是有帮助的，但有些地方（1972—1973版）则离原意太远，或有过于铺陈添凑的倾向。实际上，我更愿意参考1962年版的白话译文，因为后者更简明扼要。

张向天在鲁迅研究界出名，一方面要归因于他提出的一种解释。他认为，人们通常称为《自题小像》一诗中的"神矢"不是指"丘比特的箭"（如许寿裳和锡金以前解释的那样），而是指拜伦作品《莱拉》中的人物莱拉（Lara）死时所受之箭——"飞矢来贯其胸，遂死"——这是鲁迅1907年写的《摩罗诗力说》第四节中用的词句。无论读者是否同意他的这种分析，他无疑为这首引起了广泛争论的诗篇贡献了一种颇具创造性的阐释。一般地说，张向天的释文利大于害总是不错的。

但对他的后来者周振甫而言，就不一定能这么说了。我认为

---

① 张秉新，原是沈阳一个新教牧师的儿子，曾为香港的高中教师，后来因为他支持过圣心学校的学生抗议运动而被剥夺了公职。他在香港左派报纸《新晚报》和《大公报》上以丙公的笔名发表文章，这样靠稿费过活一直到1986年去世。他1959年和1962年发表的鲁迅诗歌注解现在仍被大陆鲁迅研究专家普遍看重。1972—1973年（时为"文化大革命"时期）的版本也还是重要的，尽管使用起来应该谨慎小心（因为加上了一些和鲁迅诗无关的内容，像当时的政治口号等）。

我们可以假设鲁迅20世纪30年代写的诗大多数都影射国统区残酷无情的统治，这是一种颇为有用的解读方式，但周振甫却竭力地将鲁迅30年代的诗作解读为国共内战的暗指，抑或竭力将之解释为鲁迅赞美共产党的苏区（内地的革命根据地）的积极诗句。最不可思议的一个例证出现在他的解读著作1962年版第77—80页，其中他把鲁迅《湘灵歌》中的悲剧情调，扭曲为乐观的胜利之歌，是在欢呼红军反围剿斗争的胜利。该书1980年版第141—144页，他解释作于1932年12月31日的无题诗《洞庭木落楚天高》时，将其中的"眉黛猩红浣战袍"一句，看作鲁迅对郁达夫提出一种父亲般的建议，希望他不因迷恋王映霞，而抛开摆在自己面前的重大任务——他刚刚开始的成为一个革命作家的生涯（周把"眉黛"释为眼部化妆，把"猩红"当作为唇膏的颜色）。

　　周振甫因为对毛泽东主席诗词的篇幅浩大的注释而知名。因此之故，詹纳尔在外文出版社出版的译本大部分依靠周注就不令人吃惊了。[①]周振甫声明，他是在张向天著作的第一版（1959）出来时开始动笔起草的，并觉得自己的注释与张向天的注释有很大不同，他认为，应该把其间的异同交给读者去审核和判断（第186页）。但他的注解建立在1981年注释本《鲁迅全集》基础上，而且几乎是逐字逐句的照搬，就使我不能不猜测这是周扬时代要搞出官方鲁迅诗歌注解本的一次尝试，是为了对付以前司空无忌和张向天对鲁迅诗歌的"独立"的解读。1980年周振甫的著作出了修订本，由同一家出版社出版。令人失望的是，大部分

---

① 毕竟，20世纪30年代最重要的事情（在党的八十岁以上的领导人心目中，落实到这里就是外文出版社所谓"中文编辑"的心目中）是内战，而中国最重要的地区则是苏区或曰革命根据地。但那不一定是鲁迅的看法。他当时人在上海，卷入一场性质和程度完全不同的斗争中。

新增内容试图对他的批评者进行反驳。

一部更有魅力的著作是无署名的《鲁迅诗笺选集：附诗稿》，一部很有美学眼光、很吸引人的书，郭沫若作序。总体上说，这是一部较少政治色彩的出版物，提供了一些颇有创见的看法。版式是传统的，文学典故和许多诗的语汇的解释被精细地嵌在行间，假如我要给学生们开一门鲁迅诗歌的课程，这本书应该是一个有吸引力的首选文本。

向读者介绍有关鲁迅诗歌注释的种种争论，纯粹从实用角度来考虑，值得推荐的是张恩和的《鲁迅旧诗集解》。该书从各种中国评论者的文字中摘出常常是互为矛盾的观点，篇幅较长，涉及鲁迅现存所有旧体诗。编者偶尔也提出自己的看法，前面加上"今按"二字。张恩和还在书后附了一篇42页鲁迅旧体诗研究方面的书籍和文章目录。

除了以上这些著作，从1978年以来还有至少十种独立的鲁迅旧体诗研究著作在中国大陆出版。这些诗作真的值得引起这样的关注吗？詹纳尔告诉我们："鲁迅30年代写的旧体诗差不多都是对特殊事件的回应。有时会有一个朋友，或者一个陌生人通过一个朋友求他的诗或一纸书法。大多数来求诗和字的是日本人。"（第21页）但日本学者高田淳若干年以前这样说：

> 尽管作为一个朋友，鲁迅会亲笔写诗赠人，但也有的诗与受赠人无直接的联系。说这些诗只是应酬之作，是浮浅的看法。其实，他的某些作品早就构思好了，只是后来才应熟人的要求将之写出来。[①]

---

[①] 高田淳：《鲁迅诗话》，东京，中央公论社1971年版，第4页。

换言之，把鲁迅多数旧体诗说成一时兴会之作是过于简单化的，尽管他经常把自己的诗说成这样。毕竟，鲁迅是新诗（白话诗）的一个强有力支持者，他不能公开支持文言。但私下里，他写出的意见则相反：

> 我只有一个私见，以为剧本虽有放在书桌上的和演在舞台上的两种，但究以后一种为好；诗歌虽有眼看的和嘴唱的两种，也究以后一种为好；可惜中国的新诗大概是前一种。没有节调，没有韵，它唱不来；唱不来，就记不住，记不住，就不能在人们的脑子里将旧诗挤出，占了它的地位。[1]

"即兴诗"（偶尔为之）的主要问题之一是，它倾向于把所含意义琐细化，把即便不是尖刻的，当然也是批评性的诗行琐细化。关于表面上看起来是偶尔为之的诗，鲁迅本人曾在1935年2月7日给曹靖华的信中这样说：

> 这里的出版，一榻胡涂，有些"文学家"做了检查官，简直是胡闹。去年年底，有一个朋友收集我的旧文字，在印出的集子里所遗漏或删去的，钞了一本，名《集外集》，送去审查。结果有十篇不准印。最奇怪的是其中几篇系十年前的通信，那时不但并无现在之"国民政府"，而且文字和政治也毫不相关。但有几首颇激烈

---

[1] 见鲁迅1934年11月1日致窦隐夫信，《鲁迅全集》第12卷第556页。

的旧诗,他们却并不删去。

如果我们在翻译和注释过程中忽略了鲁迅本人有关这些诗的性质和含义的声明,只按"偶尔为之"的标准将这些篇什看作在记述会面、外出或宴会来翻译,我想就不是把他的诗歌当作文学作品来研究。

既然说到"偶尔为之"的问题,那么让我们来看看鲁迅1932年12月31日为滨之上(Hamanoue)和坪井(Tsuboi)两位医生做的两首无题诗。

### 无题(二首)

一

故乡黯黯锁玄云,
遥夜迢迢隔上春。
岁暮何堪再惆怅,
且持卮酒食河豚。

二

皓齿吴娃唱柳枝,
酒阑人静暮春时。
无端旧梦驱残醉,
独对灯阴忆子规。

吴钧陶译作(见译本第57页):

1

My native place is overcast with dark clouds brooding on,

And Spring is barred by the very night lasting long.

How can I keep in low spirits still when it's the year's end?

Let me enjoy the dish of globe-fish with a goblet in hand.

2

'Tis a night in late spring when wines're drained and voices cease;

A Suzhou girl sings her Willow Songs and white are her teeth.

From drunkenness I'm sobered by dreams coming from nowhere;

In the shades of light alone I think of the cuckoo somewhere.

詹纳尔译作（见译本第61页）：

1

When black clouds smother the land with darkness,

And long nights make the spring seem far away,

Let not the old year's misery increase:

So raise your wine-cups and we'll feast on globefish.

2

The white-toothed southern maiden sings a ballad

In a late spring silence when the wine is gone.

Then, for no reason, an old dream makes one sober;

Alone and out of the light I think of sorrow.

陈颖则译为（见译本第99页）：

1

Homeland, dark and gloomy, lies under a blackening overcast

In the prolonged night, early spring seems far, far behind.

At year's end, how could I still have a troubled mind?

For now: a cup of wine and globe fish for a delicious repast.

2

A maiden from Wu with snowy teeth sings a "Willow Branches" lay.

The banquet's over, voices subside, as springtime wears away.

An old dream dispels my lingering drunkenness for

no reason at all;
　　Alone facing the shadow of the lamp, I remember the cuckoo's call.

所有这些译文的一个根本问题是，它们都没能保存弥漫在原诗中的忧郁情绪。相反，他们把注意力都放在酒、女人和歌曲上。实际上，这些只是诗人沉思的背景。在第一首诗中，主人公被描绘在吃河豚——日本人和唐代的中国人视为美食——它体内有毒，如果厨师料理不当会致人死命。如果在第一首诗和第二首诗联合意象产生的意境中来读的话，很清楚这不仅仅是与日本熟人在城里一起吃饭后的即兴之作。它在指明鱼体内的毒的同时，也在指明诗人体内和心中之毒，那就是上一句中所说的惆怅。

中国诗一般是各句一起产生作用，有的是直接相加，有的是形成反衬效果。它们不是每行独立存在，正如陈颖的标点所指明的。即便吃河豚被当作一种有着梦幻色彩的活动，它也仍然有着苦涩的一面，因为要看上下文的含义："在中国，我们为什么有这样的境遇？"（这是"玄云"和"遥夜"的含义）。诗中的主人公是在问："谁造成了这种局面？它们的结果还不清楚吗？暂时的缓解怎能提供真正的摆脱？"这才是作者在诗中向中国知识界甚至扩大了说向日本知识界提出的真正问题。

吴钧陶在译这两首诗时没有为读者做任何注解说明。陈颖的脚注（第231页）也没有提到上面的意象或其隐含意义。詹纳尔告诉我们，"河豚……含有致命的毒"，但似乎没有看出用在这里有什么寓意。但高田淳在他的《鲁迅诗话》中将讲解这首诗的一章命名为《河豚的惆怅》（意即河豚象征着惆怅）。他主张，这里的吃河豚可能表明诗人心中的一种程度近似于对死的渴望的内心感受（第148页）。

如果不看中文原文，乍一读，詹纳尔的译文似乎应该最忠实于原文。但译文的第一行，他把"锁"字（to lock up）译作"smother"（窒息），没有加入一些加强这诗句的力量的东西，却把双关的可能性排除掉了。如果我们想让前两句的译文听起来更像一首诗，我建议这么译：

> My old home locked in murky clouds,
> So dark, yet ever darkening;
> On, drag on, unending night,
> That hinders the coming spring.

詹纳尔好像认为"迢迢"是指春天，但从语法上说，它修饰的是"遥夜"。[①]为什么这里把故乡直译为"old home"——和我译的一样——而很可能作者在用这个词来作为他的祖国的代称？当然这是可能的，但当这一类的信息可以放在脚注里，而原始的寓意（那在英语中也多多少少能发挥作用）被保存下来时，为什么一定要说出来呢？有一点必须注意，诗人其时并不在国外，另一点要注意的是，直译成英语时这里应该加强愤怒的情绪：即作为反对派的诗人对他的祖国也有一种权力，而且事实上是比政府的"走狗"更权威的一种。鲁迅和那些领着薪酬的政府的辩护者们一样，完全是中国的，即便他写出了尖刻的文字抨击当局，并

---

① 见高田淳著作第148页；张向天著作（1962年版）第116页。参阅周振甫著作（1962年版）第112—113页。詹纳尔采用了周振甫的白话释义（第113页）："这里说反动统治的黑暗时期还没有结束，离开大地回春的光明年月还很遥远，透露出诗人渴望解放的心情。"

且与日本人一起去饮酒。右翼对爱国并没有专有权，诗中的主人公告诉我们这一点，正如他这个时期的杂文告诉我们的那样。

在译第二首诗时，詹纳尔和陈颖把"无端"一词译为"for no reason"和"for no reason at all"，吴钧陶则译作"coming from nowhere"。这个词有特殊的诗歌用法，在英语中也许最好是不直接表达出来，如果一定要这么做，我宁愿译成"inexplicably"。诗的最后一句，詹纳尔译作："Alone and out of the light I think of sorrow"这是做了一个聪明的回避，避免译那谜一样的三个字，"忆子规"，不译作"想到了杜鹃"（recalling the cuckoo），而译作"想到了悲哀"（I think of sorrow）。但诗人不是"在光亮之外"，而是"面对阴影"（facing the shadows）。这是很清楚的。当然，诗中的主人公是悲伤的（我写所有这些也正是要说明这一点），而詹纳尔正确地向我们指明了这一点。但中文原文以另一种方式在起作用，在三个译者中，①只有陈颖试图给出一个解释（第231页）：

> 中国文献中子规鸟的名字是个拟声词。其叫声听起来像"不如归去"。注意，那个"规"字与"归"字谐音。在暮春里听到这叫声，传统上与忧郁和思乡相关联。这种鸟在中国诗里还有其他几个广为人知的名称……

在中国，杜鹃这种鸟的名字有象征意义，与一个传说相关联。据说这种鸟叫声听起来像"不如归去"，可以在旅行者心中引起剧烈的思乡之情。鲁迅这里选择一个较不普遍被使用的名字

---

① 可再比较一下，高田淳著作第149—152页，他把这一整章都叫作"忆子规"。

"子规",取其与"归"字的谐音,而不用更为广泛使用的"杜鹃",也许是要加强其象征意义,表达回到什么地方去的渴望。《鲁迅诗笺选集:附诗稿》(第92页)认为诗人仍然怀着回到北京去的愿望。另一些会把这地方说成日本。但倪墨炎(第152页)和周振甫(第113页)都认为鲁迅使用杜鹃所取象征意义与屈原在《离骚》中使用时的象征意义是一样的,屈原的诗句是:

> 恐鹈鴂之先鸣兮,
> 使夫百草为之不芳。

倪墨炎和周振甫解释说,杜鹃的叫声引起香草枯萎,亦即使好人受害或遭不幸。周振甫得出结论说,诗人在为反动派践踏有才能的人而叹息,而倪墨炎说这行诗是在怀念被杀害的革命烈士。做一个对比是颇有趣的。张向天认为这首绝句的每一行的主人公都是那个歌女本人,而不是鲁迅。这就是詹纳尔发表如下评论的来源(第140页):

"另一种释义是可能的:即歌女离开了灯下,突然清醒了。"张向天认为最后一句表达的是一个母亲在盼望她的儿子归来,她儿子在"一·二八"与日本人的冲突中丢失。姜添表达了第五种释义,认为这里说到杜鹃是在用古代周时期蜀(今四川)国统治者杜宇的故事。传说中,杜王变成了一只杜鹃,洒泪成血。南宋诗人文天祥(1236—1283)有一句诗,就用这个意象表达悲剧英雄的命运:

> 化作啼鹃带血归。[1]

---

[1]《文天祥全集》,中国书店,1985年版,355页。

由此立论，姜添认为这里的杜鹃象征"烈士的忠心"。无论这种释义最终会是怎样，随意地忽略这个意象和其多义性，把这一行译作"Alone and out of the light I think of sorrow"，却是不正确的，"忆子规"显然是在用一个典故。其次"独对灯阴"也不像詹纳尔所说的主人公走出了灯光区。如果要押韵地译这首诗的后两行，我想这么译：

> A tipsy mood now chased away,
> As dreams lurch from the past;
> Alone, recall a cuckoos form
> 'Mid shadows the lamp's cast.[①]

这样译，使主人公没有特指，就像在中文中一样，而且保存了原诗所有的一些神秘的情绪。也许会有人争辩，这里的典故原本用的是杜鹃的声音，而不是形体，但诗人并没有明确告诉我们这一点。也许，诗人面对灯影，想象在其中造出了一种形体，并由此在读者心目中产生出与这种鸟的忧郁的叫声有关的象征性联想。

鲁迅的诗善用典故和寓意，这一点只要看一看他现存的最早的那首通常被人称作《自题小像》的七绝，就很容易明了。这首诗可能做于1903的春天或夏天。这也许是鲁迅被人整体引用最多的一首诗，但对其寓意却有各种不同的解释，其写作日期也不确定，甚至它这个最常用的题目也非他本人所定，而是别人给取的。中国

---

[①] 这里的lamp's等于lamp has（缩略形式），请比较我的无韵体译文：Inexplicably, dreams from the past Drive away the last of my tipsiness. Alone, facing the shadows cast by a lamp, I call to mind a cuckoo. 见《中国文学：短论、论文和评论》第3卷第1期第187页。

大陆给这首诗定的重大意义可以从下面这个事实中看出来：它常被引用来作为鲁迅思想分期即鲁迅"革命"意识起点的证据。[1]

自来这首七言绝句的大多数标准释义都遵从着鲁迅的老朋友、浙江同乡许寿裳（1883—1948）指引的路线：

> 首句说留学外邦所受刺激之深，次写遥望故国风雨飘摇之状，三述同胞未醒，不胜寂寞之感，末了直抒怀抱，是一句毕生实践的格言。[2]

但许寿裳关于本诗写作时代背景和写作地点的几个说法自相矛盾。[3]这些说法也与鲁迅晚年重抄这首诗时提供的信息不一致，那个抄本的落款是这样："二十一岁时作，五十一岁时写

---

[1] 但以前的解释有不同。有一位鲁迅生平的研究者假定这首诗和鲁迅1904年决定在弘文学院毕业后去学医有关。写这首诗如何表现年轻的鲁迅介绍医治疾病从而拯救他的人民。这是王冶秋的《民元前的鲁迅》（上海，峨眉出版公司，1947年版，第81—82页）。一个有很大差异的版本来自锡金，他说，许广平1941年曾向他解释过这首诗中几个隐晦词句的含义。按许广平的说法，这首诗表达了鲁迅对自己不得不屈从包办婚姻的忧闷。但一直到1907年，鲁迅的母亲才以生病为借口，把他从日本召回绍兴完婚。见锡金：《鲁迅诗本事》，《文学月刊》，1956年第11期第9页。

[2] 许寿裳：《我所认识的鲁迅》，北京人民文学出版社，1952年版，第24—25页。

[3] 例如，1936年，许寿裳写道："鲁迅对于民族解放事业，坚贞无比，在一九〇三年留学东京时，赠我小像，后补以诗，曰：……"见《我所认识的鲁迅》第4页。"一九〇三年他二十三岁，在东京有一首《自题小像》赠我的：……"同上，第24页。1944年，他又说："《自题小像》是其二十三岁时赠余者。"同上，第83页。但在1947年的一篇文章中，许寿裳谈到鲁迅1904年已离开东京（不是他以前说的1903年）去往小地方的仙台医专："别后，他寄给我一张照片，后面题一首七绝诗，有……"他引述了最后一句。见《亡友鲁迅印象记》，上海峨眉出版社，1947年版，第18页。

出,时辛未(1931年)二月十六日也。"这里记年龄的"岁"没有指明是按中国的计算法还是按西方的计算法。因为有这些自相矛盾之处,我们就不能认定所有许寿裳关于这首诗的声明都是定论。但在我看来,有一点是可以接受的,就是他们两个在日本留学期间,鲁迅为许寿裳抄写了这首七言绝句,写在自己的一张照片上,而这张照片和鲁迅寄给二弟周作人的那一张一样。这张照片是1903年3月鲁迅剪掉了象征民族压迫的辫子以后拍摄的。因此威廉·莱尔把这首诗看作是"他对自己在社会上的作用意识的转折点"[①]。有关这首诗诠释的大量争论产生于诗中古词语和典故的歧义性。

陈颖和吴钧陶把"自题小像"译作"Inscription on My Photograph"和"Inscribing on a Photo of Myself"是不正确的,因为,正如我已经指出的,这首诗原本无题。现在通行的标题是在诗做成以后别人(许寿裳)定的,而不是鲁迅本人所拟。原文如下:

灵台无计逃神矢,
风雨如磐暗故园。
寄意寒星荃不察,
我以我血荐轩辕。

我本人1978年最早的"直译"是这样:

Personally Inscribed on a Small Picture
In the spirit tower is no plan

---

[①] 威廉·莱尔:《鲁迅的现实观》,伯克莱,加利福尼亚大学出版社1976年版,第58页。

to elude divine arrows;
Wind and rain, like giant flagstones,
darken the old garden.
Entrusting intentions to a lone, cold star,
... the Fragrant One considers them not.
I take my blood and offer it up
to Xuan Yuan [the Yellow Emperor].①

吴钧陶（第19页）把这首诗译作：

Inscribing on a Photo of Myself
There's no way for my heart to shun the Cupid's arrow-head,
And stormy clouds, like millstones, darken our motherland o'erhead;
I ask the meteor to carry to my people my pray;
Although they ignore, I'll offer my blood to my Cathay.

詹纳尔的译本（第31页）是：

On a Photograph of Himself

---

① 我的译文早于所有其他英语版本，但李欧梵后来却在所著书中错误地把我的译文说成詹纳尔的。见李欧梵《铁屋里的呐喊：鲁迅研究》，布鲁明顿，印第安纳大学出版社，1987年版，第13页，第202页注42，并参较詹纳尔译本第31页。李氏后来在私人信件上表示了歉意。

The tower cannot avoid the god's sharp arrows;
Dark is the ancient garden crushed beneath the storm
Unrecognized, I put my hope in an ice-cold star
While offering my blood to the Yellow Emperor.

陈颖的译文（第65页）为：

Inscription on My Photograph
My hallowed heart fails to escape the sacred arrow's aim.
A rock-like storm is darkening my native land.
A message via cool stars, the grass roots don't understand
I sacrifice my blood in the Yellow Emperor's name.

当然，因为所有中国的评论者、翻译者和解说者（我本人也一样）对这首诗的理解是不完整的，所以以上这些译文就存在一些问题。我试图给读者一种"直译"，但却不得不加许多脚注（共九个）来解释词语含义并且还加一个序言式的说明。先按下拙译存在的问题不表，我们先来看看吴钧陶的译文。吴钧陶把"灵台"译作"心"，就像高田淳的日文译文中做的那样（Sore wa Rojin jibun no kokoro o iu），这不是没有道理的，[①]因为"灵

---

[①] "这里指的是鲁迅自己的心。"见高田淳著作第17页。这里不能扩大到陈颖的"我的神圣的心"，这个可怕的词使诗中的主人公听起来像一个自我膨胀的狂人。同样，他把"荃"译作"普通老百姓"，使我更多地想到了1972年麦戈文竞选总统初期的不幸命运，而不是想到这是从中国古典诗歌中借来的词语。

台"这个词在《庄子·庚桑楚》中用来指心灵,或者说把心当作智慧的基础。《庄子》原文如下:

> 备物以将形,藏不虞以生心,敬中以达彼。若是而万恶至者,皆天也,而非人也,不足以滑成,不可内于灵台。灵台者有持,而不知其所持而不可持者也。①

上面这段话,就其把"灵台"解释为从属于有意识的判断的心灵而言,与这首诗有关。因为有意识地和深思熟虑地决定参加反清革命事业,作者意识到他正要把生命献出来,结果可能会"忍受暴虐的命运的毒箭"。如果清廷真这么想,它的特务就会在日本将他逮捕,送回中国审判,还可能被绞死。那样一来,第一句中他声明的他个人的自我保存的含义就不存在争议了。②

但也可以把灵台解释为周文王的灵台(《孟子》),③那是文王的忠实的追随者建造来表达他们对模范君王的赞美的。在这种语境中,他同慈禧太后(1835—1908)形成了对照,后者用原本拨给海军使之现代化的款项建造了颐和园。因此,当诗人说"无计逃神矢"时,他指的是慈禧太后的奢侈浪费使国家丧失了防御能

---

① 我对这一段的解读依据陈鼓应的《庄子今注今译》,北京,中华书局,1983年版,第607—608页,参见伯顿·吴兹生译《庄子全书》,纽约,哥伦比亚大学出版社,1968年版,第254—255页。沃森在这段后边加注释道:"灵台如同灵府,存放灵魂的地方,是道教词汇,指心灵……"
② 见倪墨炎著作第42页,参较《鲁迅诗歌选注》,《北京师范大学学报》1976年5—6期,第109—110页。
③ 见《孟子·梁惠王》上,詹姆斯·理雅各译本《中国经典》,香港大学出版社,1960年版,第二卷,第128页。理雅各最后把"灵台"译作"marvellous tower",早期的译本则直译为"spirit tower"。

力。这是曾敏之的观点。

鲁迅的故乡绍兴城外正好有一个古迹叫轩辕台。轩辕是传说中汉民族的祖先黄帝的名字。因之灵台也可以指诗人的家乡，扩大了说，指他的祖国。处在危难中的祖国是本诗第一句的精髓所在。它符合逻辑地引向了第二句中的风雨摧残的故园（也就是故家）。但这样一来神矢的释义就落空了。大多数评论者对神矢一词的释义以许寿裳1944年的释义为基础，他是这么解释的：

> 首句之"神矢"，盖借用罗马神话爱神之故事，即异域典故。①

以上的解释达到的总体结论是"丘匹特的箭在青年鲁迅心中激发了强烈的爱国热情"（倪墨炎，第40—42页）。但丘匹特的箭只造成男女两人之间的情爱，而不是像中文里所说的爱国感情。天使射出一箭让一个人情愿为国家或革命事业而死，这样的意象显得太不协调。尤其是如果考虑到那个小爱神对于战争和武器是那么厌恶，以致他让阿波罗迷上达芙妮主要是因为阿波罗的好战倾向使爱神不快。鲁迅当时正研读"拜伦的诗、尼采的传、希腊神话、罗马神话等等"②，很有可能知道这些细节。

这就是张向天提出他的释义时所持的论据。他认为神矢的形象可能是从拜伦的《莱拉》③中女主人公莱拉的死法中来的。从鲁迅1907年写的《摩罗诗力说》中可以清楚地看出，他认同拜

---

① 许寿裳：《我所认识的鲁迅》第83—84页。
② 许寿裳：《亡友鲁迅印象记》，第5页。
③ 见张向天著作1962年版，第35页。

伦这类诗人和莱拉"力抗不可避之定命"的形象上表现出来的"撒旦式"的不服从和反叛精神。张向天认为鲁迅诗中提到的这种箭正像出乎意料地射中莱拉胸膛的箭。因此，按张向天的说法，"神矢"中神这个字含义就不是"神圣的"，而是"神秘的，隐晦的，深不可测的，无法预料的……"（第35页）也许正因为如此詹纳尔自己的译文中磨出了"尖利"（sharp）一词。

吴钧陶把寒星译为"流星"（meteor）并不错，因为这正是这个词的古意之一。寒星所在的这一行〔字面意义是"寒冷的星"，引申义为孤星（lone star），或流星（shooting star）〕，使人想起《楚辞·九辩》中的诗句，其中就用的是流星，而不是鲁迅诗中用的"寒星"。《九辩》原文是（有大卫·霍克斯 David Hawkes 译本）：

愿寄言夫流星兮，
羌倏忽而难当。①

（I wished to send my message by a shooting star,
But he sped too fast, and I could not catch up with him.）

公元2世纪王逸注《楚辞》，认为流星隐喻仍然留在政府中的正人，遭谗被逐的诗人屈原可以通过他们传递信息给他的故国楚国那位被迷惑被欺骗的君王。②我认为，在鲁迅的诗中，寒星同样可以用来比喻那些真诚、有改革志向的忠心于清朝的保皇

---

① 见大卫·霍克斯《楚辞：南方之歌——古代中国诗集》，牛津，克莱伦登出版社，1959年版，第98页。
②《楚辞补注》，四部备要本，第8卷，第13页正面。

派,他们住在日本或海外其他地方,可以作为进步分子的中间人,把后者的改革想法转达给皇帝;或者,在当前这种场合,是在比喻北京清廷掌权者。[1]这样,这句诗就是在指明所有这些努力的虚空和无效。

与其在"my pray"(应该是 prayer)和"Cathay"(这类强行押韵在吴钧陶的译本中并不少见)这些枝节问题上絮叨,还不如多把时间花在詹纳尔的译文上,他对这首诗的翻译似乎最有可能忠实于原著。第三句中的"荃不察",源于《离骚》。荃是一种香草,用来隐喻诗人的国君。大卫·霍克斯写道:

> 这里用的中文字"荃"是一种花名,一般被看作与蝴蝶花或蒁(灯芯草)同类,在这里上下文中,通常暗指诗人的国君……
>
> 《离骚》明显地包含一些隐喻。愤怒的芷,退步的兰,椒似佞人,兰芷容易变心,等等("余以兰为可恃兮,羌无实而容长……""椒专佞而慢……""兰芷变而不芳兮,荃蕙化而为茅"等等),如果不是隐喻的话就毫无意义了……
>
> 在我看来,毫无疑问,这里的"荃"是指诗人的国君……[2]

鲁迅很可能想起了被废黜的光绪皇帝,但我更倾向于认为他是在指一般意义上的中国当权者。这里很明显有对政治形势的评

---

[1] 参阅《鲁迅诗笺》。
[2] 《楚辞——南方之歌》,第212—213页。

论,或至少有对如何治理国家的思考。因此詹纳尔译作:"unrecognized, I put my hope in an ice-cold star"不但在句法上扭曲变形,而且把"荃不察"(詹纳尔只简单译为 unrecognized)的重心转移到诗人身上,听起来就像他在对自己人生的不如意感到很懊恼。第四句开始译者用的"while"也打乱了时序,因为,从语法上说,第四句或者可以作为第三句的结果,或者至少也应该直接紧跟第三句,而不是平行的。

这首诗,一直到第三句还用的是古典词汇,就在最后一句中突然使用接近于白话的词句,用了"我以我血"这个短语。这种突兀的对照使读者震惊,明显达到了卒章显志的效果。"我"这个词突进来使抽象的述说有了新的切近的指陈。在谈到绝句这种诗体的技巧时,霍克斯很早以前就指出:

> 在其他语言中情形似乎也是这样,诗的简短增加了对最后一句的强调。中国诗人写绝句,刻意把最后一句写得震撼、吸引人甚至迷惑人,使读者在结束阅读以后很长时间能继续思考和品味。①

这样,诗的最后一句更可以被视为理解其他意象的锁钥。而当出现疑问时,最好还是在文本内部找到线索,因为一首诗毕竟有它的自身结构——主题的完整性。

在鲁迅的诗中有很多这样的例证,我们这里不能一一列举讨论了。以上例证只是用来说明陈颖所说的(第30页)鲁迅诗歌

---

① 大卫·霍克斯:《袖珍杜甫读本》,牛津,克莱伦登出版社,1967年版,第186页。

"索解为难"的原因。看了上述几种不同的英文译文，给我留下的印象之一是，吴钧陶的译本——尽管英文有缺点——还有陈颖的译本，都是出于热诚的用力之作，但对詹纳尔的译本就很难这么说了，特别是当他要读者"信得过译诗的质量"（第21页）的时候；他把鲁迅早年一些诗作称为拼凑别人的"摘句"（第19页），而他的译文经常过于简单化，在遇到现存的不同释文时却又甩手不管（"这方面仍有喋喋不休的争论……"第127页）。

相比之下，我更欣赏陈颖译本对所译对象倾注的热情。但他把鲁迅的旧体诗按"形式"划分（他把它们简单区分为两大类：古体诗和律诗），严格地说，是没有必要的，这样容易给读者造成迷惑，让他们把编年顺序弄乱。例如读者会感到纳闷，为什么1932年和1933年的诗《教授杂咏》[①]放在《别诸弟》（作于庚子年即1900年）之前，书中却没有做任何说明。

而且，陈颖译本的韵脚，固然比吴钧陶的要少一些勉强拼凑的痕迹，但有时却显得熟俗，容易使带有沉郁情绪的旧体诗听起来像肤浅的打油诗。这里举一个例证，是鲁迅1934年5月30日为日本友人新居格作的无题诗：

> 万家墨面没蒿莱，
> 敢有歌吟动地哀。
> 心事浩茫连广宇，
> 于无声处听惊雷。

---

[①] Potpourri of Professors，这是《教授杂咏》四首的可怕的译名。如果想把这个题目译得滑稽有意味，我建议译为"Diverse Versifying on Professors"。

陈颖是这么译的（第135页）：

Thousands of faces, doomed with gloom, into the wilds submerge;
Who would dare to shake the earth with a wailing dirge?
My heart with immense concerns has this vast land to enwrap.
Where silence reigns, listen for a startling thunder-clap.

读完他的译文，问题就很明显；但对陈颖教授的译文要做出公正的评价的话，我必须得说明，吴钧陶的译文（第95页）不如陈颖译文准确，而听起来比陈颖的更糟糕：

Thousands of people fall down in the wilds;
They are tattoed and condemned to death.
Yet who dares to show his grief profound with wails
And laments that would shake up the great earth?
How vast and remote my heart turns over,
That to the universe it straight wanders.
Now in the dead silence I hear ever:
Come swelling the roaring rumbles of thunders!

詹纳尔的译文（第87页）尽管避免用韵，而且还被魏璐诗特地用作例证来赞扬，仍然有把中国诗的声调琐细化的倾向：

> The gaunt-faced commoners are buried by weeds;
> None dares to sing a dirge to move the earth to grief.
> When thoughts spread wide to fill the whole of space,
> Amid the silence comes the crash of thunder.

鲁迅原诗中没有哪个地方包含了与"平民"（commoners）这个词意义相近的内容。这纯粹是詹纳尔添加的，让人不快地想起那（用詹纳尔自己的话来形容的）"不愉快的年月里"，解释者"过分简单化……试图把20世纪30年代鲁迅所有的诗作的意义都描述成装腔作势的战斗姿态"①。

陈颖对"新诗"的翻译，我相信，比他对旧诗的翻译更成功。陈颖的英文比吴钧陶的英文水平要高得多，而他的引言更直接地讨论了诗歌和翻译的形式问题，这一点又比詹纳尔的译本强。

詹纳尔译本的主要问题是，它读起来好像是一本应约而作的书，是在做一件他本来并不情愿做的事，这就使人想起北京外文出版社这些年来的工作方式，它是一间"关着门营业的店铺"。它同学者和译者订立著书或译书合同，而这些人对题目也许并不熟悉甚或并不喜欢，只因为主事者觉得在某个时候有必要出一个某种著作的英译本。而这些往往是政治决策：詹纳尔原来不是一个坏译者。最终，他的译本很可能比另外两种译本销行更广，而且被有些读者视为"官方译本"，但在某种程度上，我们必须问

---

① 詹纳尔译本第26页。

一问我们自己：这种做法是不是我要称之为整个对鲁迅遗产的"琐细化的过程"的一部分，这正是许广平和其他一些人曾指责的20世纪50年代以后中国国家机构对之进行的那种诠释。如果鲁迅的社会和文化批评蕴含的意义仍然过于遥远而不至于造成当局不快的话，那么，对待他的最好的办法似乎是简单地将他处理的问题和处理问题的方法琐细化。

从一个非西方视角来看，陈颖和吴钧陶的英文译本都使用了韵脚，是很有趣的，尽管这会不可避免地使许多读者稍一浏览就掉头而去。自从20世纪20年代亚瑟·威利（Arthur Waley）用自由体来翻译诗歌变得极为流行以来，大多数译者学他的榜样，英语世界的读者习惯性地认为所有中国诗的译文都应该是这个样式。不过，这种感情对很多能阅读和写作英文的中国学者来说是完全不能接受的，他们一直在不惜任何代价试图向我们证明：翻译成有韵诗，保存原文的形式是很重要的。也许我们最好注意这一点，因为一种以文化价值观为基础的反对意见似乎在此。

在这种情况下，人们会奇怪，为什么中国大陆控制的出版机构如香港商务印书馆这样重要的出版社上马像"新译丛"这样代价高昂的项目，其中有吴钧陶的杜甫译本和其他来自中国大陆翻译者的译品，而没有任何人来对他们的译文进行编辑加工？[①]与此形成对照的是，同样是这家香港商务印书馆，却请了像张隆溪这样的著名学者审阅了该社出版的专为中国读者编辑的欧洲著名

---

① 上海外语出版社标明吴钧陶的译本第一次印刷印数为20,000册，其中大部分都卖给了那些为学英语而急于得到中英文对照读物的年轻读者，真令人哭笑不得。

书信的英译本。① 一位《中国文学：短论、论文和评论》的编辑有一次对我说，这可能是因为他们不相信国外有什么人真会拿英文对着看。现在我相信了，他们对这一点根本就不在乎。

［原载《中国文学：短论、论文和评论》（*Chinese Literature: Essays, Articles, Reviews*）第13期，101—108页，此次翻译，作者做了修订。］

---

①《名人书信一百封》，香港，商务印书馆1986年版，为"一百丛书"之一种。

# 编 后 记

黄乔生

我最近编辑鲁迅诗歌手稿,有小序一则,其中说:"鲁迅虽以小说杂文名家,然实乃一诗人也。观其六十余首新旧体诗,或沉吟,或呐喊,嘉孺子,哀妇人,悼老友,思贤者,激发想象,震撼心灵,佳句迭出,脍炙人口。鲁迅无意以书法名家,其书写乃日常工作必须,非技艺之炫露。或将感怀时事、抒发心志之作书赠友人,寄托心意而求知音;或抄写古人名篇,浇胸中之块垒。文采飞扬,字体端正,动静圆融,充满张力。"鲁迅的诗歌,尤其是旧体诗,很受读者喜爱。

本书的译者是现任澳大利亚新南威尔士大学中文系主任的寇志明博士(Jon Eugene von Kowallis),一位鲁迅旧体诗的爱好者、研究者。寇先生本是美国人,少年时期接触鲁迅著作,在哥伦比亚大学学习中文,在檀香山夏威夷大学获得硕士学位(曾任该校东西文化中心研究员),后在伯克利加州大学攻读博士学位,其间曾到中国北京大学访学。寇先生沉潜鲁迅研究有年,成绩斐然。他的硕士论文包括对鲁迅旧体诗的注释和翻译,是当时外国文中最全的一本。几年后,他对大部分译文做了修改,出版了《诗人鲁迅：鲁迅旧体诗全英译注》一书，包括一篇总序，各诗的题解，拼音字母索引，词汇索引，书中有大量的注释。封面图案用的是曹白的木刻鲁迅像，台静农先生题签。此书出版后，寇先生进而想了解鲁迅在旧诗坛的前驱，遂以《清末民初的"旧派"诗人》为博士论文题目，研究对象主要是王闿运、樊增祥、易顺鼎、陈衍、陈三立、郑孝胥等。在研究过程，他曾请教过钱锺书、钱仲联、夏志清等前辈学者。

翻译和研究中国旧体诗，对一位外国学者来说，颇具挑战性。鲁迅的诗歌虽然并不晦涩难懂，但古典、今典很不少，暗示影射也常见，理解起来先就不易，移译成另外一种文字，更其艰难。然而，过程越艰难，收获也就越大。寇先生做鲁迅旧体诗的翻译研究，其啃硬骨头的精神，令人感佩。因为下的功夫大，他的鲁迅旧体诗英译本，在很长一个时期里，是鲁迅旧体诗最全的译本，在我看来，也是最具有学术功底的译本。

然而，在中国，寇先生的译本不大为学术圈外的读者所知。中国通行的鲁迅诗集译本是外文出版社和几家地方出版社的版本，既不全，也颇多讹误。这是很遗憾的事。

寇先生研究鲁迅旧体诗，可谓独辟蹊径。他没有翻译鲁迅的新体诗。鲁迅在五四新文化高潮中写过新体诗，但如他自己所说，那是为了配合文学革命运动，以白话作诗，算是敲敲边鼓，很快就洗手不干了。他后期的诗歌创作以旧体诗为主。鲁迅这一代人经历了新旧转换时期。新旧变化并非突然、截然，而是一个渐变过程，是一个融化和扬弃过程。只把鲁迅当作一个新文学家来认识，而不注意他们这一代人的传统文化深厚修养，就不能对他们有全面了解和正确评价。寇先生在《微妙的革命：清末民初"旧派"诗人研究》中分析同光体、唐宋诗派等诗人的作品，提出了自己的观点——这些诗人和作品不像以前人们说的反动、倒退、造假古董,而颇具现代意识。鲁迅是这些诗人的晚辈,其诗句屡有与前辈诗人灵犀相通之处。

寇先生从鲁迅旧体诗这个门径进入鲁迅研究,在有些人看来可能是旁道支路,但我觉得是正路。他完成博士论文后,转向鲁迅早期思想研究,翻译了鲁迅四篇文言论文:《摩罗诗力说》《文化偏至论》《破恶声论》《拟播布美术意见书》——他即将出版的著作《精神界之战士》在鲁迅著作的翻译、注释史上也将会独树一帜。中外不少鲁迅专家,如李欧梵、刘禾、王斑、胡志德、汪晖、慕维仁等,都在自己的著作引用过他的初稿。这说明,寇先生选作论题的鲁迅早期这些论文,在研究鲁迅思想方面有重要和恒久的价值。实际上,他多年前就曾提出这样的论点,但当时引来不少反对意见。

如此说来,寇先生研究汉学,鲁迅特别是鲁迅的旧体诗,可算是一个枢纽。其体现方式之一,就是他的鲁迅旧体诗英译。因此之故,寇先生很看重这本书。当我提出编辑中英文对照的鲁迅旧体诗集时,寇先生慨然应允,并写了长序。

我结识寇先生,始于翻译他有关鲁迅旧体诗英译的论文。这篇论文对当时流行的几个鲁迅诗歌英译本做了批评,也谈了他自己翻译过程中的感想。后来他对德国译者顾彬等人的鲁迅诗歌德文译文有所论列,我也做了介绍。我觉得寇先生的文字质朴而切要,不张扬,不虚夸。他论作家作品,总是从生平事迹出发,以注释解读为基础,有理有据,不托空言。我喜欢他的文风。

寇先生翻译鲁迅诗歌时,先将诗意直译出来,然后进行意译,着重表达其情绪和意义,字斟句酌,既注意形似,又追求神似,因此,他的译文意义准确,诗味也浓。

寇先生从实践上升到理论,对鲁迅旧体诗,特别是对鲁迅旧体诗英译中存在问题进行了系统的探讨。本书特地收录他的一篇相关研究文章,以见其深厚学养之一斑。

中国的旧体诗并没有消失,它活在鲁迅这样的新文化人物笔下,至今仍然活在中国语文里,而且,还活在像寇先生这样的喜爱中国文化的外国人的著译中。

2015年5月5日于北京

# Editor's Notes

Huang Qiaosheng

Recently I compiled another book of Lu Xun's poetry written out in his own distinctive calligraphy, to which I added a short dedication, which reads in part: "Although Lu Xun is best known for his fiction and essays, he was, at base, a poet. An overview of his poetry in the old and new styles yields line after line of beautiful verse, some pained and deeply philosophical, others decrying injustice or urging on resistance, encouraging children, decrying the plight of women, mourning fallen friends, or commemorating the virtuous men and women of our modern history, many of which can still capture the imagination or quicken the pulse of today's readers. Lu Xun never set out to distinguish himself as a calligrapher: wielding a traditional writing-brush was for him part of his daily work, not a path to acclaim for artistic or technical skill. At times when he was emotionally moved by or became distraught at some event that had taken place, he would take up his brush and write out a poem as a calligraphic keepsake expressing his feelings, with the wish that the person(s) to whom he presented it would identify with and share the same sentiment. Or sometimes he would copy out an ancient composition as a response to feelings of gloom and indignation that were on his mind as a result of those events. His style of calligraphy is elegant and uplifting, the characters themselves proportionate and well-balanced, their motion across the page easy-going and confident, yet powered by an inner-strength. Lu Xun's poems themselves, especially those composed in the old styles, are well-known and loved by Chinese readers.

The translator of this book Jon Eugene von Kowallis, Head of Chinese Studies at the University of New South Wales in Sydney, Australia, has displayed a long interest in and enthusiasm for Lu Xun's classical-style verse, both as a literary scholar and a translator. He hails originally from the United States, where he began reading Lu Xun's works at a young age in English translation, then ended up majoring in Chinese Studies at Columbia University, completed an Masters degree by research and coursework in Chinese literature at the University of Hawaii (as a fellow at the East-West Center) and subsequently continued his studies at Peking University under Sun Yushi, as part of his PhD program at the University of California, Berkeley. He has since immersed himself in Lu Xun studies, where he has become widely known through his scholarship. His Masters thesis contained the first complete annotated English translation of Lu Xun's classical-style poetry into any foreign language. Some years afterward he retranslated much of the poetry, publishing it under the title *The Lyrical Lu Xun: a Study of his Classical-style Verse*, containing a general introduction, prefaces for the various poems, pinyin romanization, literal glosses, figurative translations, and copious annotations. The cover design makes use of a woodcut by Cao Bai and the calligraphy of Tai Jingnong.

Because Dr Kowallis was curious about the poetry of Lu Xun's immediate predecessors, he undertook a study of the Poets of the 'Old Schools' during the late Qing and early Republican China, which was later published as *The Subtle Revolution*. The poets studied in that work included Wang Kaiyun, Fan Zengxiang, Yi Shunding, Chen Yan, Chen Sanli and Zheng Xiaoxu. In the process of his research he consulted senior scholars Qian Zhongshu, Qian Zhonglian and C.T. Hsia, among others.

Research on and the translation of this sort of classical Chinese verse is a challenging undertaking for any foreign scholar. Although Lu Xun's poetry is not obscurantist, it is rife with allusions to ancient literature as well as references to events in his own day, and sometimes contains veiled satire and innuendo. This can make it hard to understand literally, to say nothing of translating it into a completely different language system. Thus the difficulty of the undertaking is apparent. Nevertheless, the more challenging the process, the greater the yield. Dr Kowallis' work in research and translation reflects an admirable enthusiasm in taking on difficult tasks. Because of the time and effort he devoted to the project, *The Lyrical Lu Xun* has remained, over an extended period, the most complete study, and in my opinion, also contains the translation which is of the greatest scholarly value.

Nevertheless, Dr Kowallis' translation has never been well-known in China outside of scholarly circles. The translations which have been distributed here were from our own Foreign Languages Press and several regional publishers. They are incomplete and riddled with errors and distortions. This has been a regrettable state of affairs.

Dr Kowallis' method of approaching Lu Xun through his classical-style poetry could well be understood as original and path-breaking. He did not translate all of Lu Xun's poetry, because he intentionally excluded his new-style poems from his study. In the heady days of the May Fourth era Lu Xun composed a few new-style poems, but as he himself said, that was in an attempt to encourage the nascent literary revolution, which advocated writing poetry in the vernacular. It was also a genre he washed his hands of rather quickly afterward, reverting to the classical style in his later period. Lu Xun's generation lived through an era of major transition. The transformation from old to new was not sudden and complete, it came as part of a gradual process, a process of amalgamation, developing the good and discarding the bad. Understanding Lu Xun merely as a practitioner of the new literature, without paying sufficient attention to the extent to which men of his generation were steeped in traditional culture, will result in a failure to understand him fully and to arrive at a correct historical appraisal.

In his second monograph *The Subtle Revolution: Poets of the 'Old Schools' during late Qing and early Republican China* Dr Kowallis analyzes the works of the Neo-ancient School, the School of Mid and Late Tang Poetry, and the Tong-Guang School of Qing poets and formulates his own take on them – namely that these poets and their works were not as reactionary as others had said, nor were they backsliding producers of "imitation antiques," but rather intellectuals whose works articulated a modern consciousness. Lu Xun would have been from the next generation after them, yet his poetry echoes a certain resonance with that of his predecessors.

That Dr Kowallis first entered the study of Lu Xun by means of a work on his classical-style poetry might appear to some to have been a tangential route, but I feel it was the right way. After he finished his PhD on the Poets of the 'Old Schools', he resumed his study of Lu Xun from the angle of his early thought, which led to him completing translations of four of Lu Xun's very early essays: *On the Power of Mara Poetry*, *On Imbalanced Cultural Development*, *Toward a Refutation of Malevolent Voices*, and *A Proposal for the Promulgation of Aesthetics*. His forthcoming book, *Warriors of the Spirit*, will be yet another milestone in the translation and annotation of Lu Xun's works, worthy of acclaim. Lu Xun specialists, Chinese and foreign, including Leo Oufan Lee, Lydia Liu, Wang Ban, Theodore Huters, Wang Hui and Viren Murthy have quoted from earlier drafts of Dr Kowallis' manuscript on the early essays in their own writings on Lu Xun, which I think substantiates his thesis that those essays are of seminal and lasting value in understanding Lu Xun's thought, an argument that Dr Kowallis began presenting some years ago, in the face of considerable opposition.

All this being said, it becomes apparent that the center point and lynchpin in Dr Kowallis' scholarship on China and intervention in Lu Xun studies has always been Lu Xun's old-style poetry. For that reason he has greeted the publication of this book with great enthusiasm. When I first broached the idea of a bilingual volume of Lu Xun's classical poetry in Chinese and English aimed at the readership in China that would make use of his translations, he generously agreed, producing a new introduction for the volume.

I first made Dr Kowallis' acquaintance when I translated one of his articles about Lu Xun's poetry that presented a critique of a number of other translations and editions in circulation at the time. He also articulated thoughts and ideas that had occurred to him in the process of making his own translations. Later he wrote a review of the German translations of Lu Xun's works produced by Wolfgang Kubin and others which I also introduced to the Chinese readership. I find his style straightforward and unaffected, modest and downplayed. When he discusses authors and their works, he develops his position from the facts of their lives, piecing together the history and artifacts of their era. His scholarship is based on exegesis, annotation and close-reading. Every argument proceeds according to logic and documentation, nothing relies on empty verbiage. I like this style.

His method of translation was to first make a direct translation of the poem line by line; from there he went on to a figurative translation that conveyed the mood and meaning. To that he added detailed annotations and commentary. In his choice of wording he took great care in the replication of both form and spirit. Hence his translations turn out to be accurate both in terms of conveying the meaning and rich in poetic feeling.

Dr Kowallis proceeds from practice to theory, making systematic discussions on questions arising both in the research on and translation of Lu Xun's poetry, particularly into English. This book also includes a Chinese translation of one such article to give a glimpse of the depth and range of his scholarly enquiries.

China's classical-style poetry has definitely not faded from the scene, it has been carried over into our own time by prominent figures of the New Culture Movement such as Lu Xun, and it lives on in the Chinese language today. Moreover, it lives on because of the writings by foreign scholars like Dr Kowallis, which indicate such an enthusiastic interest in the culture of China.

May 5, 2015, Beijing

## 译者　About the author/translator:

### 寇志明

曾在哥伦比亚大学、夏威夷大学和北京大学主修中国文学，在加州伯克利大学获得东方语文博士学位。现任澳大利亚悉尼新南威尔士大学中文系主任。著有《微妙的革命：清末民初"旧派"诗人》《鲁迅旧体诗研究》《精神界之战士：鲁迅早期文言论文》等。

Jon Eugene von Kowallis studied Chinese literature at Columbia, Hawaii and Peking University, before attaining the PhD in Oriental Languages from the University of California, Berkeley. He is currently chair of Chinese Studies at the University of New South Wales in Sydney, Australia and author of *The Subtle Revolution: Poets of the 'Old Schools' during Late-Qing and Early Republican China*, *The Lyrical Lu Xun*, and *Warriors of the Spirit: Lu Xun's Early wenyan Essays*.

## 编者　About the editor/compiler:

### 黄乔生

1986年毕业于南京大学中文系，文学硕士。现任北京鲁迅博物馆常务副馆长、《鲁迅研究月刊》主编、中国鲁迅研究会副会长兼秘书长。著有《度尽劫波——周氏三兄弟》《鲁迅图传》《鲁迅像传》《八道湾十一号》等，译作《巴德，不是巴迪》《漫长的诉讼》《汤姆琼斯》等。

Huang Qiaosheng received his M.A. from Nanjing University in 1986.He is currently Executive Director of the Beijing Lu Xun Museum, Editor-in-Chief of *Lu Xun Research Monthly*, Vice-President and Secretary-general of the Chinese Association for Lu Xun Studies. Major works include *After the Kalpa has Passed: the Three Brothers Zhou* (1998), *A Visual Biography of Lu Xun through Photos* (2014), *No.11 Badaowan Lane: the Story of the Residence of the Brothers Zhou* (2015). He is also the translator of *Bud, Not buddy* (1999), *A Civil Action* (2002) and *Tom Jones: A Foundling* (2004).